BABBITT

An American Life

TWAYNE'S MASTERWORK STUDIES

Robert Lecker, General Editor

BABBITT

An American Life

Glen A. Love

TWAYNE PUBLISHERS • NEW YORK
Maxwell Macmillan Canada • Toronto
Maxwell Macmillan International • New York Oxford Singapore Sydney

Twayne's Masterwork Studies No. 105

Babbitt: An American Life
Glen A. Love

Twayne Publishers
Macmillan Publishing Company
866 Third Avenue
New York, New York 10022

Maxwell Macmillan Canada, Inc.
1200 Eglinton Avenue East
Suite 200
Don Mills, Ontario M3C 3N1

Library of Congress Cataloging-in-Publication Data

Love, Glen A., 1932–
    Babbitt : an American life / Glen A. Love.
      p.   cm. — (Twayne's masterwork studies ; no. 105)
    Includes bibliographical references (p.) and index.
    ISBN 0-8057-9440-9 (hc : alk. paper). — ISBN 0-8057-8562-0 (pb :
alk. paper)
    1. Lewis, Sinclair, 1885–1951. Babbitt. 2. National
characteristics, American, in literature. I. Title. II. Series.
PS3523.E94B297   1993
813'.52—dc20
                    92-27096
                    CIP

10 9 8 7 6 5 4 3 2 1 (hc)
10 9 8 7 6 5 4 3 2 1 (pb)

Printed in the United States of America

To Jenny

CONTENTS

NOTE ON THE REFERENCES
AND ACKNOWLEDGMENTS

Let me here acknowledge my debt to the memory of Sinclair Lewis, whose long row of novels on the shelves of the Green Lake Public Library in Seattle helped to introduce another moon-calf youth to his country's literature.

I wish to thank the following for permission to reprint copyrighted material: Harcourt Brace Jovanovich for excerpts from *Babbitt* by Sinclair Lewis, copyright 1922 by Harcourt Brace Jovanovich, Inc. and renewed 1950 by Sinclair Lewis, reprinted by permission of the publisher; also *American Quarterly* for excerpts and revisions from my article, "New Pioneering on the Prairies: Nature, Progress, and the Individual in the Novels of Sinclair Lewis," *American Quarterly* 26 (December 1973), 558–77. I also wish to thank Michael E. Connaughton, editor of *Sinclair Lewis at 100: Papers Presented at a Centennial Conference*, (St. Cloud, Minnesota: St. Cloud State University, 1985), uncopyrighted, for his assistance in using material from my essay in that volume, "Babbitt's Dance: Technology, Power, and Art in the Novels of Sinclair Lewis." I am indebted, as well, to my editors at Twayne Publishers, Mark Zadrozny and Laura Glenn, who offered valuable assistance in improving the manuscript.

References to *Babbitt* used in this volume are to the readily available Signet paperback edition.

Sinclair Lewis
Arnold Genthe. Courtesy of the Library of Congress

CHRONOLOGY: SINCLAIR LEWIS'S LIFE AND WORKS

1885   Harry Sinclair Lewis born 7 February in Sauk Centre, Minnesota, third son of Edwin J. Lewis, a physician, and Emma Kermott Lewis. A generation earlier, Sauk Centre had been wild prairie land, Indian country. Young Lewis grows up with a keen sense of the recent pioneer heritage of the American Midwest, an idea that later finds its way into many of his books.

1891   Mother dies. One year later father marries Isabel Warner. Called "Harry" by his family, Sinclair Lewis is an awkward, unathletic boy who reads voraciously and is an outsider in the rough-and-tumble boy life of the village, in which his older brother, Claude, is at home. Young Lewis is active in high school as a debater, a writer, and an actor.

1902   Enters Oberlin Academy in Ohio, to prepare for Yale University.

1903–1906   Attends Yale. Contributes to Yale literary journals and edits the *Yale Literary Magazine*. Works his way to England two summers on cattle boats; on these trips begins making notes for fiction.

1906   Leaves Yale to live and work briefly at Upton Sinclair's colony, Helicon Hall, in Englewood, New Jersey, an experiment in communal living.

1906–1907   Attempts to support himself in New York by writing and editing; nearly starves. Father offers no financial support. Later, Lewis goes to Panama to find work on the new canal, but is unsuccessful. Returns to Yale, graduating in June 1908.

1908–1910   Holds various writing and editing jobs in New York, Washington, D.C., and California. Lives in Carmel, where he meets Jack London, George Sterling, and other members of the Carmel colony of artists and bohemians. Lewis later sells short story plots to Jack London.

1910–1915   Works in New York City in publishing houses and for magazines. Publishes a boys' novel, *Hike and the Aeroplane*, in 1912 under the pseudonym Tom Graham.

1914   Publishes his first serious novel, *Our Mr. Wrenn*. He marries Grace Livingstone Hegger, who, years later, publishes a novel, *Half a Loaf*, and a biographical memoir, *With Love from Gracie*, based on their relationship and marriage.

1915   Publishes *The Trail of the Hawk*. Like *Our Mr. Wrenn*, the book enjoys favorable reviews but does not sell well. With some stories he sells to the *Saturday Evening Post* for handsome fees, he is able to quit his job and devote full time to his writing.

1917   Publishes *The Innocents* and *The Job*, the latter one of his best early works, featuring a working woman as its main character. A son, Wells, is born.

1919   Publishes *Free Air*, based on a 1916 trip in a Ford with his wife, from Sauk Centre to Seattle.

1920   Publishes *Main Street*, a controversial novel that climaxes the "revolt from the village" movement in American literature, and marks, along with the World War I armistice, the end of American innocence. The small town in America, usually the seat of goodness and virtue, is flayed in Lewis's first hugely successful novel. *Main Street* has been called the biggest event in modern American publishing history. Lewis is launched into fame.

1922   Publishes *Babbitt*, another hugely controversial book and cultural event with the public and critics.

1923   Travels in the Caribbean with Paul de Kruif, who collaborates with Lewis on his next novel, *Arrowsmith*.

1925   Publishes *Arrowsmith*. This novel is another success, but one more notable for its idealism and the radical strength of its hero, medical researcher Martin Arrowsmith.

1926   Publishes *Mantrap*; in a succession of novelistic bull's-eyes during the 1920s, this is one of two misfires (the other being *The Man Who Knew Coolidge*). Refuses to accept the Pulitzer Prize for *Arrowsmith*, thus increasing the publicity surrounding the book and further establishing his position as America's most controversial author. Father dies.

1927   Separates from his wife. Publishes *Elmer Gantry*. Skewers popular religion, as he had earlier exposed the foibles of the small

Chronology

town, the businessman, and the medical profession. Contemporary revivalists and charismatic cultists are unmasked in Lewis's most shrill and unremitting satire. Of the several of his novels made into Hollywood films, this is the most notable. The 1960 production of *Elmer Gantry* wins three Oscars, including best actor for Burt Lancaster's arresting performance in the title role.

1928	Divorces wife and marries Dorothy Thompson, journalist and political analyst. He publishes *The Man Who Knew Coolidge*. Buys a farm in Vermont, but later gives it up, evidence of his attraction to nature, but also of his inability to settle anywhere for long.
1929	Publishes *Dodsworth*, the last of his five great novels of the 1920s.
1930	Receives the Nobel Prize for literature, the first American writer to be so honored. His acceptance speech in Stockholm, entitled "The American Fear of Literature," powerfully argues Lewis's conviction that Americans are afraid of any literature that does not glorify American faults and virtues, and that the serious writer in America must work alone with only his own integrity as a guide. A second son, Michael, is born.
1933	Publishes *Ann Vickers*. Lewis's great decade is over. None of his novels from this point on will have the significance or impact of his best work of the 1920s.
1934	Publishes *Work of Art*.
1935	Publishes *Selected Short Stories* and *It Can't Happen Here*. The latter is a depiction of the fascist threat in American life. It is later dramatized, as Lewis turns his attention in the 1930s to the stage.
1936	Receives honorary degree from Yale.
1937	Separates from his second wife. Lewis's difficult personality, his restlessness, and his increasing drinking problem make him a poor marriage-partner.
1938	Publishes *The Prodigal Parents*.
1939	Tours with his play, *Angela Is Twenty-Two*. Now in his mid-fifties, is involved with a young actress who later leaves him to marry someone younger.
1940	Publishes *Bethel Merriday*, a novel about a budding actress. Teaches a writing class briefly at the University of Wisconsin, leaving in mid-term.
1942	Is divorced from second wife. Does not remarry.

1943	Publishes *Gideon Planish*, a weak satire on the philanthropy business.
1944	Receives the news that his first son, Wells, has been killed in action in France during World War II.
1945	Publishes *Cass Timberlane*. The story of a middle-aged man in love with a younger woman parallels his own earlier experience.
1947	Publishes *Kingsblood Royal*. A flash of the old fire emerges in this novel as Lewis addresses the problem of racism against Blacks in the American heartland.
1949	Publishes *The God-Seeker*. William Dean Howells once claimed that a realist had no business writing historical novels. Lewis here proves the point.
1951	Dies in Rome, Italy, on 10 January, of heart disease. His ashes are returned to his birthplace in Sauk Centre. *World So Wide*, his last novel and a pale shadow of his best work of the 1920s, is published posthumously.

Literary and Historical Context

1

Babbitt and the Twenties

The 1920s, the decade of Sinclair Lewis's *Babbitt* as well as his other best-known novels, is commonly described as a shallow and materialistic period in American history. References to the "Roaring Twenties," the "Jazz Age," "flaming youth," "flappers," "speakeasies," and the like are often found in popular descriptions of these years. Perhaps because the decade is clearly marked, with World War I at one end and the 1929 stock market collapse and the Great Depression of the 1930s at the other, it has lent itself to depictions of sensationalism and uniqueness.

Like most generalizations, the depiction of the 1920s as a decade bent on self-indulgence and material pursuits is true enough, if applied selectively. In the popular culture of the twenties, as Frederick Lewis Allen points out in his influential history of the times, *Only Yesterday* (1931), there seemed to be a sense of hysteria to much of the social life of the era. The end of the war with Germany on 11 November 1918, and the subsequent wish for a return to "normalcy" was thwarted by a rush of rapid and undeniable changes in American life. The communist revolution in Russia had stirred American fears of the "Reds." Labor unrest and strikes were rumored to be evidence of a

Bolshevik conspiracy against the country, and political rhetoric was polarized in the context of a widespread fear that a worker's revolution might be imminent.

Something of this mistrust and suspicion of foreign influences could be seen in the most infamous trial of the decade, the Sacco and Vanzetti case, in which two Italian anarchists, Nicola Sacco and Bartolomeo Vanzetti, were arrested for robbery and murder. After a lengthy trial and in the absence of any convincing evidence of their guilt, they were executed. The affair became a worldwide cause, with demonstrations on behalf of the two men being held in the United States as well as in Europe and South America. Their arrest and trial became the subject of a wave of liberal and radical journalism as well as many literary works, such as John Dos Passos's trilogy, U.S.A. (1938), covering the first three decades of the century. Felix Frankfurter, later to become a U.S. Supreme Court justice, wrote of the case in 1927: "By systematic exploitation of the defendants' alien blood, their imperfect knowledge of English, their unpopular social views, and their opposition to the war, the District Attorney invoked against them a riot of political passion and patriotic sentiment; and the trial judge connived at—one had almost written, cooperated in—the process."[1] Of this trial judge, Frankfurter went on to claim that "Judge Thayer's opinion stands unmatched for discrepancies between what the record discloses and what the opinion conveys. His 25,000-word document cannot accurately be described otherwise than as a farrago of misquotations, misrepresentations, suppressions, and mutilations. . . . The opinion is literally honeycombed with demonstrable errors, and a spirit alien to judicial utterance permeates the whole" (Frankfurter, 134). Despite all such protests and appeals, the sentence of death against the two men was carried out. Equal justice before the law and protection of rights for those who espoused minority and unpopular opinions seemed to have fallen victim to a belief that radical ideas themselves were justification for state-sanctioned murder.

More widespread evidence of intolerance could be seen in the rise of the Ku Klux Klan, founded in 1915, which set itself up as the militant defender of white Aryan Protestantism, though its principal activity was the intimidation and persecution of black Americans. By

1924 its membership reputedly numbered in the millions and it wielded dominant political control in a number of states, including Arkansas, California, Indiana, Ohio, Oklahoma, Oregon, and Texas. The Klan called for "the instincts of loyalty to the white race, to the traditions of America, and to the spirit of Protestantism, which has been an essential part of Americanism ever since the days of Roanoke and Plymouth Rock. They are condensed into the Klan slogan: 'Native, white, Protestant supremacy.' "[2]

At the same time that such reactionary forces were struggling to shore up what they considered to be the eternal American verities, other trends and events seemed to announce that the older restraints on personal freedom in manners and morals were breaking down. The wide availability of radio and the growing popularity of Hollywood films were to influence the lives and attitudes of Americans as strongly as television was to do thirty years later. For the first time, everybody could hear and see virtually everything. Sports, and particularly professional sports, became a major presence in public life. Football, baseball, prizefighting, golf, tennis, and other contests played to record-breaking crowds, stirred to interest by the hero-hungry media. Along with the radio and the movies, the increasing availability of the automobile, of sensation-seeking magazines and newspapers, and the rapid growth of the new advertising industry all helped to broaden the scope of hedonistic possibilities for Americans whose private desires had been held in check by a long tradition of Puritanism. Servicemen returning from war assignment in a more open and permissive Europe chafed under the prim standards of their homes and communities, as a young returnee from the war, Ernest Hemingway, was to reveal in a story called "Soldier's Home." Tin Pan Alley song lyrics underscored the issue by demanding, in the voice of the vulgate, "How ya gonna keep 'em down on the farm, after they've seen Paree?"

The private moral standards of much of the populace seemed to demonstrate the cynical claim that the new morality was nothing but the old immorality. The traditional moral code held that women were its guardians, a single romantic love-match that led to the altar and motherhood (in strictly that order) was their sole purpose in life, and premarital sex, or even dalliance, was forbidden. A firm double standard allowed that men—weaker moral vessels that they were—might fall to the enticements of sex, but not proper young women. Among respectable families, smoking and drinking were unacceptable not only for all women but for the younger set of both sexes. Rouge and lipstick were considered the badges of prostitutes. Female dress seemed designed for the purposes of maximum concealment and minimum movement.

The end of World War I seemed to signal a revolution in such mores. The beginning of the decade of the twenties saw the hemlines of women's dresses daringly raised above the ankles. Growing numbers of aggressively unconventional young women—called flappers—defying the restrictions placed on them, wore revealing clothes, danced athletically, even frantically, to fast, sometimes syncopated "ragged time" or "ragtime" music, or "jazz," and used make-up. Many of them smoked cigarettes, kissed more men than the one they were to marry, and drank hard liquor—even though the Eighteenth Amendment to the Constitution, the "prohibition amendment," passed in 1919, had made liquor illegal. While Prohibition was repealed in 1933, its existence in the twenties, along with a booming trade in the outlawed manufacture, import, and sale of alcoholic beverages, served to mark the air of hypocrisy and evasion between official utterance and actual behavior that has come to characterize the decade. F. Scott Fitzgerald was to catch the spirit of rebellious youth and especially "fast" young women in his first novel, *This Side of Paradise* (1920), and in his short stories of the times collected in *Flappers and Philosophers* (1920) and *Tales of the Jazz Age* (1922).

Not all of the changes in moral behavior were of a frivolous nature. The growing independence of American women was marked by their gaining of voting rights in 1920, establishing at long-last their political equality with men. More and more, women were entering the labor force, unwilling to be bound by the traditional role of housewife, or by the limited fields customarily open to them, such as teaching and nursing. While the question of whether married women or mothers had a right to work was still a hotly debated issue in the twenties, there was little question that a career was appropriate for unmarried women. Sinclair Lewis had pioneered the story of the working woman in the heroine, Una Golden, of his 1917 novel, *The Job*. He was to dramatize the frustration of the questing woman more memorably in the figure of Carol Kennicott in his first great novel success, *Main Street* (1920). Throughout the 1920s women threw off the constraints that had bound them to proscribed lives and narrowed opportunities.

Sexual relationships between men and women, as portrayed in books and drama, were treated, in the 1920s, with new frankness. Since the turn of the century, when books like Theodore Dreiser's *Sister Carrie* (1900) and Kate Chopin's *The Awakening* (1899) had met a wall of resistance to their honest and serious treatment of sex, audiences and publishers had changed. Though Chopin had been silenced by the outraged public reaction to *The Awakening*, Dreiser continued to challenge sexual hypocrisy in America in his serious writing after 1900. By the time he published his masterwork, *An American Tragedy* (1925), sex could be dealt with more openly in American fiction. With Dreiser and H. L. Mencken clearing the way, as novelist and critic, respectively, the path to greater sexual honesty had been opened for the younger generation of American writers, as Hemingway's *The Sun Also Rises* (1926) served to demonstrate. With the memory of a recent president in the White House (Warren G. Harding) whose not-too-private life included many sordid sexual encounters and—according to his mistress—the fathering of an illegitimate daughter, novelists could no longer be admonished for taking undue liberties.

If a puritanical sexual morality lost something of its hold on the public during the 1920s, so too did conventional religion. While church membership continued to grow at about the rate of population increase, the depth of commitment on the part of the faithful seemed less assured. The new God was science, and technology was its uncontradictable proof and prophet. Machines were revising the lives of Americans, from the home to the workplace, in systems of commerce, transportation, medicine, information, entertainment—everywhere. Driven to a smaller and smaller sphere of influence, organized Christianity was forced to choose between allying itself with the new science, or denying it in favor of a literal interpretation of the Bible. Those who took the latter course, calling themselves "Fundamentalists," found themselves held up to public examination in the famous Scopes trial in Dayton, Tennessee, in 1925. A young high school biology teacher in Dayton, John Thomas Scopes, was placed on trial for teaching evolution in his classroom, a practice forbidden by action of the Tennessee state legislature. With ex—secretary of state, presidential candidate, and Populist folk-hero William Jennings Bryan as chief spokesman for the prosecution, and Clarence Darrow, an agnostic and the country's most prominent legal defender of radicals, as Scopes's lawyer—and with famed critic, journalist, and gadfly of middlebrow America H. L. Mencken covering the action, along with a phalanx of other reporters—the Scopes trial became a cultural happening of major symbolic importance. The affair was to be memorably dramatized in the 1955 play by Jerome Lawrence and Robert E. Lee, since filmed by Hollywood, *Inherit the Wind*.

Though the Scopes trial resulted in a nominal victory for the prosecution and the old-time religion, Fundamentalism had been held up to worldwide attention and had been found increasingly irrelevant, even the object of derision, in the age of an assured and triumphant science. Sinclair Lewis followed the Scopes trial with another of his blockbuster novels, *Elmer Gantry* (1927), in which organized religion in America, from the backwaters of Fundamentalism to the urban temples of the charismatic religionists and practitioners of Higher Thought, is pierced by the arrows of Lewis's most withering satire.

The counterpart of this attack on religion is seen in Lewis's defense of—even deification of—the new science, in his novel *Arrowsmith* (1925). While *Arrowsmith* exposes much of the pettiness and self-serving within the medical profession, it treats pure science as mankind's noblest work, and its practitioners like Max Gottlieb and Martin Arrowsmith as true modern heroes.

Arrowsmith serves to remind us of the seriousness of the responses of artists and intellectuals in the 1920s to a social order characterized by political and personal hypocrisy as well as by the suppression and persecution of aliens, minorities and women, on the one hand, and by a mindless pursuit of pleasure and diversion on the other. For many of the younger American artists and intellectuals, such a cultural climate stimulated a response of rejection and revolt.

Babbitt *and the Twenties*

Harold Stearns brought together the opinions of thirty—mostly younger—American intellectuals in his anthology *Civilization in the United States* (1922), and noted a common theme: American society was hostile to art and intellect, and there was little hope for improvement in that regard. One recourse recommended by Stearns's contributors for those who would practice the life of the mind was to get out of America, to become expatriates. Among those who had already made their escape was Ezra Pound, poet and critic, born in Idaho in 1885, the year of Lewis's birth, and raised in Pennsylvania. Pound had gone to Italy in 1908, and from there and elsewhere in Europe served as something of a model and guide for those who found American life inimical to their work and thought. Especially in his long poem *Hugh Selwyn Mauberley* (1920), Pound was an important influence on younger writers, many of whom, such as T. S. Eliot, Ernest Hemingway, F. Scott Fitzgerald, Robert McAlmon, Katherine Anne Porter, Glenway Wescott, and Kay Boyle, followed his example in becoming expatriates, of long or short duration. For those who went to Paris, a popular destination for the young artists, there was the freedom to live as one would, and for very little money. There was a community of like-minded, creative people, and informal salons and gathering places for young artists, presided over by literary figures like Ford Madox Ford and Gertrude Stein. There was Sylvia Beach's bookshop, frequented by an Irish writer, James Joyce, whose work proved to be highly influential, and by many of the American writers.

Even though Sinclair Lewis was always a wanderer, and something of an expatriate himself—especially in the latter half of his life, he does not really belong with the younger writers such as Joyce, Hemingway, Fitzgerald, and Dos Passos, who were to produce the great modernist texts of the 1920s. As Malcolm Cowley points out in his definitive study of the literary expatriates, *Exile's Return* (1951), these were young people who graduated from college, or might have graduated, between about 1915 and 1922, and who felt "a sharper sense of difference in regard to writers who hadn't shared their adventures. It was as if the others had never undergone the same initiatory rites and had never been admitted to the same broad confraternity. In a strict sense the new writers formed what is known as a literary generation."[3] Sinclair Lewis must have felt this difference keenly, for in his Nobel Prize acceptance speech in 1930, he generously cited the work of a number of the younger American writers "who are doing such passionate and authentic work that it makes me sick to see that I am a little too old to be one of them."[4]

Lewis was thirty-five and had been writing professionally for a decade or more before he achieved success with *Main Street* in 1920. The writers more contemporary with him are those who suggest less the spirit of the twenties than that of the first two decades of the century, writers like Theodore Dreiser, Sherwood Anderson, and Willa Cather, who had done a good deal of their best work before 1920 and the arrival on the scene of the bitter youths of the "lost generation." Thus, Lewis wrote his best books and achieved his fame in a decade that has, in the literary histories, seemed almost to exclude him. It is perhaps more useful, then, in evaluating his work and the ideas that inform it, to consider him as being influenced by the late-nineteenth century spirit of Utopian idealism (as revealed in Edward Bellamy's immensely popular *Looking Backward* [1888]), and the Progressive political heritage of the turn of the century, when Lewis was just coming to maturity. Lewis parallels the social agenda of the Progressives in his attempt to give individual form, in the body of his works, to the great formlessness of early modern American life. After a post–Civil War period of rapid growth and movement of population, of bewildering technological advancement, of the conversion of his native Midwest from an agricultural frontier to a city-dominated industrial empire, Lewis appears consciously to attempt to order the social and moral confusion that characterized the ascendant new America. The confusion seems compounded in a novel like *Babbitt*, where, as William E. Leuchtenburg describes the 1920s in *The Perils of Prosperity* (1958), an economy of scarcity is being transformed into one of abundance.

The ambivalent desires of Lewis's characters to both participate in, and withdraw from, the society shaped by the new forces of urban industrialism were shared by the Progressive political movement during the years of its greatest influence, from 1890 to 1920. Lewis and many of his literary characters frequently seem to reflect the Progressive belief that society might respond to leadership along innovative and ameliorative lines, and that new emblems of possibility were needed to overcome the sense of crisis and failure which, as evidenced in the so-called muckraking investigative journalism, was widespread at the turn of the century. Like the Progressives, Lewis and many of his characters project the hope that Americans could subsume the city and machine civilization into the traditional democratic framework without sacrificing pastoral values. Like the Progressives, Lewis and the figures in his novels are firmly in thrall to the cities, and identify with their professional class and role in modern life, yet long for the simplicity and sweetness of nature and the countryside.

Lewis's novels and the lives of many of his most significant characters may also be seen in the historical context of pioneering. While Harold Stearns had, in his indictment of American culture in *Civilization in the United States*, singled out the pioneer as a chief source of American intellectual sterility (the pioneer being identified with anti-intellectualism, pragmatism, and disdain for art and beauty), Lewis had a much more positive conception of American pioneering, born out of his sense of his own western heritage. Lewis's work reflects values that are largely frontier and pioneer inspired, with a heroic view of the past and an essentially hopeful and progressive conception of the future. Out of the awareness of the swift conversion of his own upper-Midwest country from agrarian frontier to machine civilization arises Lewis's sense of the myriad possibilities for individual human lives. The apprehension at the swiftness of change, versus the still-unextinguished belief in actual progress, the newness and heterogeneity of the western populace versus the sense of its interconnections with the more established East, and the encroachment of the city on the land versus the continuing sense of nature as the wellspring of meaningful values—these are the representative conflicts of Lewis as a Progressive and a westerner.

While Sinclair Lewis accepted with part of his mind the vitality and urgency of the new America, he hesitated to commit himself and his characters fully to it. In the argument surrounding this ambivalence there is much of Lewis, and of Babbitt—both the novel and the man.

2

Capturing the Archetype

English-language dictionaries include an entry for "Babbitt" that reads something like the following: "A self-satisfied person who conforms readily to middle-class attitudes and ideals. [After the character in *Babbitt*, a novel (1922) by Sinclair Lewis.]—Babbittry *n*."[1]

While any careful reader of the novel must question the judgment that Babbitt is wholly self-satisfied, or that he conforms readily, the presence of the word "Babbitt" in the lexicon of the English-speaking world is evidence of the widespread and pervasive impact of Lewis's novel. A few years after Lewis's novel was published an English writer, C. E. M. Joad, entitled his harsh indictment of American civilization *The Babbitt Warren* (1926). More recently, Elizabeth Stevenson called her history of the 1920s *Babbitts and Bohemians* (1967). And, as Joseph Wood Krutch pointed out, "Babbitts defending babbittry used the term with which he [Lewis] had supplied them."[2] Even when the term "Babbitt" was withheld, its influence could be seen behind nearly every image of American conformity in ensuing years, including those presented in such well-known books as Sloan Wilson's *The Man in the Gray Flannel Suit* (1955), William Whyte's *The Organization Man* (1956), and David Riesman's *The Lonely Crowd* (1961).

What does it mean for a writer to have lodged a new noun in our common vocabulary? It means that a name has been given to that which people recognize and accept as true to their experience of life, but which they hadn't realized in any palpable way, for up to that point there had been no word for it. The English writer H. G. Wells caught this quality in *Babbitt* when he wrote to Lewis to praise his new novel, saying " 'Babbitt' is what we call a 'creation' but what we really mean is that he is a completely individualized realization of a hitherto elusive type."[3] American novelist John O'Hara emphasized the point more recently, saying "All the other novelists and journalists and Babbitt himself were equally blind to Babbitt and Zenith and the United States of 1922. Do you know of anyone since Fielding who made such an important discovery-creation, and without a war for a backdrop?" (Schorer 1961, 351).

One delight of literature is that it gives coherent shape to the hitherto shapeless and unrecognized meaning of our experience. Kenneth Burke tells us that form, in art, is the arousing of an expectation in the mind of the audience—and then the fulfilling of that expectation. In a realistic work like *Babbitt* the expectation already exists, to some extent, in the common experience of the audience. But it is the writer's art that starts with the familiar and the random, and makes it new and meaningful. Every teacher of the novel Babbitt, if my own experience is typical, has encountered students who, in quiet moments after class, or in conference, confide that in George F. Babbitt they recognized for the first time in fiction an unerring portrait of a father or an uncle or a friend. The literary worth of *Babbitt* is that it resonates within us, like a myth or an archetype. It gives form to a widely shared sense of life, but one that has previously only been partially perceived and never articulated. *Babbitt*, like Robert Frost's description of poetry, surprises us with what we didn't know we knew.

The importance of *Babbitt* might be said to begin with its resonating realism. It is a hugely detailed book that chronicles with startling clarity the era of the 1920s, described in the previous chapter. Within the pages of *Babbitt* one finds revealed, through character and action, the urge toward "normalcy" and business as usual in postwar America, the fear of socialists and "Reds" and labor unrest, the suspicion of

363 3006

foreigners and "radical" ideas, the suppression and denial of non-WASP culture, the rebellion of the young, the siren appeal of bohemianism, the continuing lure of nature, the monumental hypocrisy of Prohibition, the influence of the mass media and advertising in shaping public desires, the aridity of women's lives, the decline of religion (both in the commercialization of the polite churches and in the pugnacious ignorance of the Fundamentalists) the newly ascendant gods of science and technology; all of these exist in a context of conformity that is at once both comforting and suffocating. This is the Babbitt of the dictionary term, the universal emblem of the Solid Citizen, stuffed with the clichés of his class and calling, possessed by his possessions.

If *Babbitt* is a memorable work of realism, it also continues to attract readers because it is a significant work of satire. While it shows us much of American middle-class life, it is stylistically distinguished. It is a very funny book that deftly punctures the presumptuousness of an entire age and class of people. Satire has tended to run to the toothless rather than the biting variety in America, say the critics. Our national preference, we are told, gravitates more to humor—good-natured joshing—than to the acid wit of satire. While our greatest comic writer, Mark Twain, was capable of withering satire, he was never loved for it in his own times, nor in ours, for that matter. Much of Twain's most devastating satire was either suppressed by him or ignored by his readers. It is as a humorist that he is best remembered. And an unremittingly waspish and thoroughgoing satirist like Ambrose Bierce, roughly contemporary with Mark Twain, was never a popular favorite. Nor was Lewis's contemporary and champion H. L. Mencken, whose satire, too erudite for the common herd who were its targets, found its readers among the like-minded intelligentsia.

But Lewis was different. He was the first major American writer to be both popular and a satirist. Lewis gave the American public vinegar and made them like it. Having learned his techniques from the realists, he often uses dialogue to show rather than tell, thus letting his victims impale themselves. As Vernon L. Parrington said of Lewis, "He ingratiatingly makes up to George F. Babbitt of Zenith, drinks chummily with him, swaps greasy jokes, learns all the hidden vanities and secret obscenities that slip out in the confidences of the cups, beguiles him into painting his own portrait in the manly midnight hours; and when the last garment that covers his nakedness is stripped off, the flashlight explodes and the camera has caught the victim in every feature of his mean and vacuous reality."[4]

Parrington's metaphor of the camera shot here reminds us of the familiar critical judgment against Lewis that his talents are only in catching snapshot likenesses, in mimicry. Take the scene in *Babbitt* when T. Cholmondeley ("Chum") Frink, Babbitt's "literary" friend who makes his living writing poems for the newspapers, is eyeing the pitcher of contraband cocktails at Babbitt's party:

> Chum Frink, a traveled man and not unused to woes, was stricken by the thought that the potion might be merely fruit-juice with a little neutral spirits. He looked timorous as Babbitt, a moist and ecstatic almoner, held out a glass, but as he tasted it he piped, "Oh, man, let me dream on! It ain't true, but don't waken me! Jus' lemme slumber!"
>
> Two hours before, Frink had completed a newspaper lyric beginning:
>
> I sat alone and groused and thunk, and scratched my head and sighed and wunk, and groaned, "There still are boobs, alack, who'd like the old-time gin-mill back; that den that makes a sage a loon, the vile and smelly old saloon!" I'll never miss their poison booze, whilst I the bubbling spring can use, that leaves my head at merry morn as clear as any babe new born![5]

This may be typical Lewis mimicry, but it is mimicry of a rare and high order. It not only skewers the hypocrisy of the Frinks and Babbitts who privately delight in their sins while sanctimoniously upholding the official virtues of Prohibition in public, but it also ridicules the bonehead popular mentality that elevates Chum's doggerel "po-emulations" to the status of art. And yet this offhanded juxtaposition and ludicrous versifying is so outrageous as to be delightful to the reader. *Babbitt* is rich with such material. It may be called "mere mimicry," but let those who can write so cleverly cast the first stone. There is clearly more than mirroring going on here, as the selection and arrangement and creation evident in even this brief example reveal.

And without the mimicry, how would we know the world of the 1920s so well, for who but Lewis had the ear and the eye to take it all in and get it all down?

But *Babbitt*'s significance does not end with its realism and satire. The book's unusual success also lies within the character of Babbitt himself, which reveals something more than can be conveyed through realistic reportage and the lampooning of the age. Lewis himself noted Babbitt's shadow side in a notebook entry on the novel: "He is too tragic a tyrant for the puerilities of deliberate satire. And he is an individual, very eager and well-intentioned, credulous of pioneering myths, doubtful in his secret hours, affectionate toward his rebellious daughter and those lunchmates who pass for friends—a god self-slain on his modern improved altar—the most grievous victim of his own militant dullness—crying in restless dreams for the arms of Phyrne."[6] Lewis finds George F. Babbitt worth more than ridicule because of Babbitt's dreams, his hopes, the poignant realization of his own lost life. There is something durably human and solid about Babbitt after all. He desires something he does not understand, as do a great many of the other figures in the book. What that something is, the ill-formed but insistent idealism that lies beneath the targeted superficialities, is worth pursuing further. Where is the urban figure who will shape into assured and memorable form the ascendant technology that Babbitt so helplessly admires and serves? How can the latent spirit of pioneering, of democratic optimism and progressive reform, embody itself in the isolated army of restless yearners that Babbitt personifies?

When the Swedish Academy awarded the Nobel Prize for literature to Lewis in 1930, the first American writer to be so honored, they specified that their decision finally came down to the excellence of the single novel, *Babbitt* (Schorer 1961, 543). While the motivations of the Academy have been the subject of much speculation and analysis, it seems undeniable that for the judges in 1930 *Babbitt* was Lewis's masterpiece, a definitive work in the accession of American literature to world status. Is it any less today?

3

Babbitt and the Critics

While the phenomenal success of *Main Street* in 1920 was still in full swing, Lewis was hard at work on his new novel which was to become *Babbitt*. In November, 1920 Lewis wrote to critic Carl Van Doren,

> Already I am planning a second novel of the same general sort as "Main Street," though utterly different in detail. It is, this time, the story . . . of an Average Business Man, a Tired Business Man, not in a Gopher Prairie but in a city of three or four hundred thousand people (equally Minneapolis or Seattle or Rochester or Atlanta) with its enormous industrial power, its Little Theater and Master of the Fox Hounds and lively country club, and its overwhelming, menacing heresy hunt, its narrow-eyed (and damned capable) crushing of anything threatening its commercial oligarchy. I hope to keep it as far as may be from all "propaganda"; I hope to make that man live—that man whom we have heard in the Pullman smoker, ponderously lecturing on oil stock, the beauty of Lake Louise, the impertinence of George the porter, and the excellence of his 1918 Buick which is so much better a model than the 1919.[1]

This suggests the realistic and parodic qualities of the new novel as it was taking shape in Lewis's mind. Another side of the emerging character of Babbitt, though, was to reveal itself later, in a letter Lewis wrote to his publisher, Alfred Harcourt. Babbitt, said Lewis, "is all of us Americans at forty-six, prosperous but worried, wanting—passionately—to seize something more than motor cars and a house *before it's too late*. . . . [H]e would like for once the flare of romantic love, the satisfaction of having left a mark on the city, and a let-up in his constant warring on competitors. . .√. I want to make Babbitt big in his real-ness, in his relation to all of us, not in the least exceptional, yet dramatic, passionate, struggling."[2] This idealistic strain, so much like the thwarted aspirations of Carol Kennicott in *Main Street*, was to emerge unmistakably in the final portrait of Babbitt when the book was published on 14 September 1922.

After *Main Street*, it is not surprising that *Babbitt* was eagerly awaited by critics and readers. What *was* surprising was that, for many in this receptive audience, *Babbitt* had outdone even the earlier success of *Main Street*. May Sinclair sounded a characteristic note in her review in the *New York Times Book Review* when she wrote that in *Babbitt*, "Mr. Sinclair Lewis triumphs precisely where in *Main Street* he failed. By fixing attention firmly on one superb central figure he has achieved an admirable effect of unity and concentration. Not once in all his 401 close-packed pages does your gaze wander, or desire to wander, from the personality of George F. Babbitt (of the Babbitt-Thompson Realty Company)." May Sinclair also called attention to the remarkable appeal of the main character, "so lovable and so alive that you watch him with a continuous thrill of pleasurable excitement." She concluded her review with the wry observation that "though nobody will recognize himself in George F. Babbitt, everybody will recognize somebody else."[3]

Upton Sinclair, author of *The Jungle* (1906) and founder of the socialist community at Helicon Hall in New Jersey, to which young Lewis had fled as a college student, announced, "I am now ready to get out in the middle of the street and shout hurrah, for America's most popular novelist has just sent me his new book, and it is a scream. I am here to enter my prediction that it will be the most talked about and the most read novel which has been published in this country in my life-time."[4] Stuart Sherman, professor of English at the University of Illinois, added the approval of the academic establishment when he wrote, "Sinclair Lewis is conspiring with the spirit of the times to become the most interesting and important novelist in America."[5]

The liveliest and most significant send-off for *Babbitt*, though, was from the influential critic H. L. Mencken. Mencken had met Lewis briefly, at a social gathering, before the publication of *Main Street* made Lewis famous. In that brief encounter, Lewis had seemed to Mencken a ridiculous figure, a carrot-topped loudmouth, a nobody who announced to Mencken and the others present that he had just written a novel that was to give complacent middle America the jolt of its life. When *Main Street* was published, Mencken's scoff turned to astonished admiration. The red-headed boaster had actually done it! Here were Mencken's favorite targets—America's joyless and conformist puritanism, its hatred of genuine beauty and art, its crass commercialism, its pious moralism—all brought to life in an electrifying new novel. From that point on through the 1920s, Mencken became Lewis's critical champion. When *Babbitt* appeared, Mencken wrote for the *Smart Set* a stunning review entitled "Portrait of an American Citizen." Opening with the claim that *Babbitt* was "at least twice as good a novel as *Main Street* was," Mencken delighted in the satiric reality of Babbitt's character:

> The fellow simply drips with human juices. Every one of his joints is movable in all directions. Real freckles are upon his neck and real sweat stands out upon his forehead. I have personally known him since my earliest days as a newspaper reporter, back in the last century. I have heard him make such speeches as Cicero never dreamed of at banquets of the Chamber of Commerce. I have seen him marching in parades. I have observed him advancing upon his Presbyterian tabernacle of a Sunday morning, his somewhat stoutish lady upon his arm. I have watched and heard him crank his Buick. I have noted the effects of alcohol upon him, both before and after Prohibition. And I have seen him, when some convention of Good Fellows was in town, at his innocent sports in the parlors of brothels, grandly ordering wine at $10 a round and bidding the professor play "White Wings."[6]

After cataloging, in his own bumptious style, the achievements of *Babbitt*, Mencken concludes that in all of the book's details and scenes "there is more than mere humor; there is searching truth. They reveal something. I know of no American novel that more accurately presents the real America. It is a social document of a high order" (Mencken, 22).

Babbitt's popular and critical success continued through the decade, with the words "Babbitt" and "Babbittry" passing into the language, as we have seen, as synonyms for middlebrow conformists and conformity. The novel was filmed twice by Hollywood, in 1924 and again in 1934, though neither production was to match the cinematic excellence of later films from Lewis books like Dodsworth and Elmer Gantry.[7] As a novel, Babbitt set a high standard against which Lewis's forthcoming novels were measured. Critic Joseph Wood Krutch, for example, called his review in the Nation of Lewis's 1927 novel Elmer Gantry, "Mr. Babbitt's Spiritual Guide" (reprinted in Schorer 1962, 36–38). By the end of the 1920s, with a string of big novels, including Babbitt, to his credit, critics were viewing Lewis's work in archetypal terms. T. K. Whipple likened Lewis to a "Red Indian in the enemy's country. His eye is always alert and keen for inconsistencies or weaknesses in his prey—and how quickly he pounces!"[8] For Constance Rourke, in her landmark study, American Humor, Lewis was in the tradition of American fabulists: "The material is prosaic, the mood at bottom romantic; gusto infuses the whole, with an air of discovery. Even the derision is not a new note; this had appeared again and again in American attitudes toward American life, and is part of the enduring native self-consciousness; it is seen here, as before, in a close tie with the comic. . . . Babbitt takes a place beside the archetypal Yankee, and for the first time an archetypal native scene is drawn in Main Street." Rourke concludes that, in his absorption of the detail and scene of American life, "Lewis may be considered the first American novelist."[9]

Something of this opinion was obviously behind the decision of the Swedish Academy to name Lewis in 1930 as the first American writer to receive the Nobel Prize. In choosing Lewis over Theodore Dreiser and other American writers, the Academy was most impressed by the typicality and representativeness of Lewis's fictional creations, and by the artistic and affirmative qualities in Lewis's work, as well as its more notorious satire and critical realism. These qualities, the

Academy believed, had raised American literature to a place among the world's literature. And *Babbitt* was acknowledged as the apex of Lewis's achievement.[10]

If 1930 saw Lewis at the top of his career—he had just completed a remarkably creative decade, having produced five very important novels capped by the Nobel Prize—that year also marked the beginning of a decline in Lewis's performance as a writer and in the critical estimation of his work. Lewis, of course, had always had his detractors, many of whom, like Sherwood Anderson, were constitutionally unable to appreciate the braying, caustic quality of even a *Main Street* or a *Babbitt*. But with a string of novelistic successes behind him, with H. L. Mencken riding shotgun to keep the hostiles at bay, and with the big prize in hand as testimony to the world's esteem, Lewis ended the decade of the 1920s in a position so lofty that it could not be maintained. " 'This is the end of me,' " he is reported to have said after hearing that he was to receive the Nobel Prize. " 'This is fatal. I cannot live up to it' " (Schorer 1961, 543).

The following decades were to prove that his fears were not unfounded. His novels of the 1930s and 1940s were never to recapture the potency and energy of his best earlier work. A list of their titles— *Ann Vickers, Work of Art, The Prodigal Parents, Bethel Merriday, Gideon Planish, Cass Timberlane, Kingsblood Royal, The God Seeker, World So Wide*—reads today like a roll call of Sumerian kings, as Mencken once said of the assembled novels of William Dean Howells. Mencken himself ceased to be a major critical force in the 1930s, as his increasingly reactionary, anti-government politics and firebrand rhetoric ran counter to the sober economic realities of the Great Depression and the social reforms of Franklin D. Roosevelt and the New Deal. In any event, there was not much in Lewis's new novels to excite Mencken's admiration.

T. K. Whipple, in his 1928 assessment of Lewis, noted approvingly Lewis's satirical and realistic gifts, but also sounded the note of dispraise that was to become characteristic of criticism and reappraisal of Lewis in the years to follow: "While many of his [Lewis's] contemporaries, who have succeeded in maintaining their integrity unimpaired, import to their readers an intenser realization of the world they live in, the net result of Lewis's work is not a truer apprehension or a deeper insight, but an increase in mutual dissatisfaction. . . . Lewis is the most successful critic of American society because he is himself the best proof that his charges are just" (Whipple 1928, 228). By 1942, in his influential literary history of modern American prose literature, *On Native Grounds*, Alfred Kazin saw Lewis, like Sherwood Anderson, as someone who had outlived his talent. Anderson, "the drowsing village mystic," and Lewis, "the garrulous village atheist" had, after early triumphs, shared a common humiliation, that of "being remembered as 'cultural influences' rather than as serious and growing artists; of knowing that they had ceased to be significant, or even interesting, after seeing their first works go so deeply into the national mind and language."[11] For Kazin, Lewis's novels were less than art, "not so much revelations of life as brilliant equivalents of it," and his later works revealed the decline of his mimetic gifts into the mere repetition of a trick (Kazin, 175, 179).

This largely unfavorable reappraisal of Lewis's work was typical of critical response as literary modernism, with its antimimetic, antirealistic assumptions came to dominate literary tastes in the mid-twentieth century. Mark Schorer's massive biography of Lewis, *Sinclair Lewis: An American Life*, published in 1961, continued the pattern of modernist and new critical disparagement of Lewis's achievement. Nevertheless, Schorer's book set a new high standard for literary biography, and is by far the most important scholarly tool in dealing with Lewis's life and work. Schorer concluded, like Kazin, that Lewis was important as a cultural influence, that he was a major force in liberating American literature, and that he created characters "that live now in the American tradition itself." Still, his works are often artistic failures. "He was one of the worst writers in modern American literature, but without his writing one cannot imagine modern American literature" (Schorer 1961, 813).

For many admirers and critics of Lewis, Schorer's judgments were unreasonably negative, and suggested an antipathy toward the writer that left the biography's final judgments open to question. Jack L. Davis offered his analysis of Schorer's negativity in a challenging 1971 essay. Davis notes that since the publication of the biography, Schorer had retreated somewhat from his disparaging stance. In his 1969 essay on *Babbitt*, Schorer had, according to Davis, taken a critical position more capable of treating Lewis's achievements fairly.[12]

A tendency to give greater attention to Lewis's strengths as a writer is evident in the book-length critical studies of Lewis that have come out since the Schorer biography in 1961, such as those by Sheldon Grebstein (which argues sensibly against those who lessen Lewis's value by lumping his good books with his bad), D. J. Dooley, James Lundquist (who persuasively balances Schorer's depictions of Lewis's tormented youth), Richard O'Connor, and Martin Light. Robert E. Fleming's 1980 bibliography, *Sinclair Lewis: A Reference Guide*; Michael E. Connaughton's collection from the Lewis Centennial celebration, *Sinclair Lewis at 100* (which includes additions to Fleming's bibliography to 1985); and Martin Bucco's 1985 *Critical Essays on Sinclair Lewis*, bring the student of Lewis nearly up to the present. Bucco's book contains a useful introductory survey of Lewis's career and critical reputation, and reprints representative criticism.

A check of the items listed under "*Babbitt*" in Fleming's *Reference Guide* reveals that *Babbitt* continues to attract a number of critics. The book has been linked to a wide range of other works, including Homer's *The Iliad*, Dante's *Inferno*, Pope's "Rape of the Lock," Mark Twain's *The Gilded Age*, William Dean Howells's *The Rise of Silas Lapham*, Dreiser's Cowperwood novels, Edith Wharton's *The Age of Innocence*, Arthur Miller's *Death of a Salesman*, Kurt Vonnegut's *Player Piano*, and J. F. Powers's *Morte d'Urban*. M. Gilbert Porter adds John Updike's *Rabbit* novels to the list in a lively recent essay.[13]

Lewis's best work, as represented by *Babbitt, Main Street, Arrowsmith, Elmer Gantry*, and *Dodsworth*, continues to occupy a distinctive place in American literary history, though not the position predicted for him by respondents to a magazine poll in 1937 that asked, "What ten American authors now living do you think have the best chances of being considered 'classics' by the reading public in the year 2000?" Sinclair Lewis's name led all the others' (Schorer 1961, 626).

A Reading

4

Babbitt and Realism

With his influential review of the new Lewis novel, *Babbitt*, H. L. Mencken announced that he knew of no American novel that more accurately presented "the real America." While it may seem odd that a work like *Babbitt* would need defending for its presentation of the *real*, such may be the case now. For in the past two or three decades, we have seen many writers and literary critics turn away from literary realism, defined by René Wellek as "the objective representation of contemporary social reality."[1]

In place of realism, many writers now pursue such literary techniques as neofabulism, magical realism, absurdism, and metafiction. They write "antinovels," or present various experiments in a language that reflects back on itself rather than on some external reality. Critics, similarly, pursue theories of nonrepresentational language and the indeterminacy of meaning. Thus, many writers and critics, at least those most favored in academic circles, seem to have concluded that writing words on a page, or reading them from a page, is the only reality. For them, life away from the book has ceased to qualify as real.

How did this view come into ascendancy, and how does it affect our reading and thinking about a novel like *Babbitt*? At the base of the antirealistic conception of the world is an attribute of language: the lack of a direct correspondence between words and their referents, the things that the words represent. Since words are not the same as their referents, all attempts to fix an absolutely "real" meaning are flawed. By a considerable theoretical extension of this linguistic observation, reality itself is called into question, and so are the concepts of meaning and reason that accompany one's sense of reality. Such denials of the real world, for all their theoretical and logical ingenuity, have not gone unchallenged. For example, nature writer Edward Abbey responds to this pattern of thinking by saying, "to refute the solipsist or the metaphysical idealist all that you have to do is take him out and throw a rock at his head: if he ducks, he's a liar. His logic may be airtight, but his argument, far from revealing the delusions of living experience, only exposes the limitations of logic."[2] It is not recorded whether rock-throwing has actually taken place. Certainly it has not appreciably thinned the ranks of the antirealists among today's writers and critics.

Added to the theoretical attractions of antimimesis (antirealism), there are its social attractions. As the political radicalism of the 1960s faded, what Gerald Graff calls the "cultural radicalism" of more recent times has grown in its place.[3] Perhaps the main feature of this cultural radicalism, according to Graff, is a rejection of objective rationality in favor of a romantic conception of the human imagination. This has resulted in a special privilege being accorded to creativity, to fantasy, to human liberation of all sorts. Realism or objectivity is seen as cultural repression, or an oppression of the liberated sensibility. In addition, some Marxist critics have tended to disparage realism because they disapprove of its middle-class subjects and readers. (Ironically, a novel like *Babbitt*—which satirizes middle-class America—may thus find itself ignored today by Marxist critics who would share many of its attitudes and assumptions.)

No one, certainly not the modern-day writer or critic, wishes to be consigned to the "middle class," to appear old-fashioned or "conservative," to be cast in a repressive or oppressive role, or to be seen as opposing the spirit of innovation and unconventionality that drives the modern system of artistic production and consumption;

realistic writers like Sinclair Lewis, and readers and critics who assume some sort of objective basis in reading and interpreting a novel like *Babbitt*, have, thus, found themselves in a no-win position. As Graff sardonically points out, "If you are looking for truth in your interpretations, you are probably longing for some kind of theocratic authority to relieve you of the anxiety of choice. Start believing in the existence of an objective world or text, and the next thing you know you will be calling out the ideological police—demanding censorship and suppressing disagreement. At the very least, you convict yourself of existential cowardice" (Graff, 18).

Realism has actually never been popular with intellectuals. A disregard for the existence of matter has always been a kind of qualification for theoretical and philosophical thought. In his famous nineteenth-century essay, "Nature," Ralph Waldo Emerson quoted Turgot to the effect that those who have never doubted the reality of the world have no aptitude for metaphysical thinking. Emerson adds approvingly that intellectualism "fastens upon . . . Ideas; and in their presence we feel that the outward circumstance is a dream and a shade."[4]

But the realist proceeds from an admittedly antitheoretical base. In answer to the disparagers of the real, the realists would find no basis for denying reality when all their experience of the world serves to affirm it. There may be free play for the artist's own system of imagination in dealing with the solitary and inner life of himself or one of his characters. But in describing a closely organized society, the individual imagination must acknowledge the existence of another system whose workability and whose involvement of so many other people is its own powerful corroboration. As J. P. Sterne puts it, realism is concerned with "the system that works."[5] Common social experience affirms reality and our shared participation in it. In the last seconds of a close basketball game, for example, the spectacle of the crowd offers convincing evidence that what we see and experience as real is indeed so. As the game-winning shot drops through the net and the final buzzer sounds, there are wild shouts and leaps from the winners, groans of anguish from the losers. What are the opportunities here for the metaphysicians? There might indeed be opportunities here for the moralist, reflecting, for example, on the sort of society that takes a sporting event so seriously. But there is nothing to prevent realists from being moralists. In fact, with a writer like Lewis the two functions are inextricably bound together, as we shall see later.

Realists might take their definition of reality from contemporary novelist Philip K. Dick, who says, "Reality is that which, when you stop believing in it, doesn't go away."[6] According to Sterne, "the realistic writer (unlike one who sets out to describe realism) has no contribution to make to any discussion about 'models of reality,' for he has no doubt about the singularity of the world in which he lives, in which we all live. . . . What [realism] implicitly denies is that in this world there is more than one reality, and that this denial is in need of proof" (Sterne, 54).

As for the linguistic argument that the lack of a direct correspondence between words and things is evidence that all attempts to fix meaning are bound to fail, the realist might counter that the existence of ambiguity doesn't prevent the real world and its language from getting along quite well enough. Despite the absence of a direct connection between a word and its referent, there *is* a referent. The world and its functions may defy exact linguistic containment, and may change over time, but they do not cease to exist. Some attempts at control, whether linguistic or "objective," are more successful than others. Some achieve power and influence; others do not. This is what interests the realist.

Words, for the realist, are real enough to get the job done. They are adequate equivalents to the social system under study. The realist rejects the notion of language as a metaphysical flight in pursuit of ungraspable phantoms, or a modernist retreat into isolated consciousness and private meanings, or a postmodernist collapse or exhaustion of meaning. One might draw an analogy here between the dictionary and the realist's perception of the significant commonality of contemporary social life. The dictionary records the commonality of verbal experience by grouping the range of acknowledged meanings that have accrued for each word. These meanings are described. Synonyms are given and the different shades of meaning between them are presented. With the dictionary, readers and writers do quite well at achieving shared understanding. While writers are free to take liberties with this shared linguistic understanding—and regularly do so, with irony, puns, reversals, ambiguity, and so on—the underlying system of coherence is not thereby destroyed. Indeed, it is, in a sense, strengthened and confirmed, for without it there would be no way for the variations to make any sense. So "the system that works" in the fact and acuality of the everyday world is represented for the realistic writer by a coherent pattern of words and sentences that also works, a system of meaningful prose.

One contemporary writer who disputes the antirealist tendencies of recent years is Tom Wolfe. In a widely noted literary manifesto published at the end of the 1980s, Wolfe assaulted the practitioners of unreality and called for a new social novel: "at this weak, pale tabescent moment in American literature, we need a battalion, a brigade of Zolas to head out into this wild, bizarre, unpredictable, Hog-stomping Baroque country of ours and reclaim it as literary property."[7] Not surprisingly, it is Sinclair Lewis whom Wolfe cites as the model for American writers to follow in summoning up a new realism. Wolfe attributes America's position in modern literature to its realistic writers, pointing out that nearly all of the Nobel laureates from the United States, since Lewis, have been realists. He argues that the decline of modern letters in America may be traced to its flight from reality, from "material," and into interior and nonmimetic worlds.

> Dickens, Dostoyevski, Balzac, Zola, and Sinclair Lewis *assumed* that the novelist had to go beyond his personal experience and head out into society as a reporter. Zola called it documentation, and his documenting expeditions to the slums, the coal mines, the races, the *folies,* department stores, wholesale food markets, newspaper offices, barnyards, railroad yards, and engine decks, notebook and pen in hand, became legendary. To write *Elmer Gantry,* the great portrait of not only a corrupt evangelist but also the entire Protestant clergy at a time when they still set the moral tone of America, Lewis left his home in New England and moved to Kansas City. He organized Bible study groups for clergymen, delivered sermons from the pulpits of preachers on summer vacations, attended tent meetings and Chautauqua lectures and church conferences and classes

at the seminaries, all the while doggedly taking notes on five-by-eight cards. (Wolfe, 52)

In emphasizing the importance of Lewis's exhaustive search for material for *Elmer Gantry*, Wolfe serves to call attention to the methodology of Lewis's realism. While Lewis's subject in *Babbitt*, American business life, had been treated previously in American literature—in novels like Howells's *A Modern Instance* (1882), *The Rise of Silas Lapham* (1885), and *A Hazard of New Fortunes* (1890); in Frank Norris's *The Octopus* (1901) and *The Pit* (1903); and in Theodore Dreiser's *The Financier* (1912) and *The Titan* (1914)—no writer before Lewis had given readers so close and so comprehensive a picture of the commercial world and its inhabitants. In writing *Main Street*, Lewis had had his own early life experiences in Sauk Centre to provide him with his material, but with *Babbitt* Lewis began the method he was to follow in his later books. This method included full familiarization with the field and the setting of the book—through carefully recorded interviews, reading, listening to speeches, attending conventions, and preparing full summaries of the plot and structure of the story. In writing *Babbitt*, Lewis also added detailed maps of the imaginary Zenith, the city in which the novel is set, and even the floor plan for Babbitt's house.[8]

This kind of immersion into the life of his projected books has led critics to term Lewis a kind of literary sociologist of American life. The appellation is not undeserved. *Babbitt* incorporates not only a keen analytic description of social setting and character, but also much of the radical sociology of Thorstein Veblen, whose books—particularly *The Theory of the Leisure Class* (1899)—first brought to public awareness such ideas as conspicuous consumption and the relationship between status, money, and social competition. This intellectual network of ideas is given unique reality by Lewis as we meet Babbitt and his household in the opening chapter and follow him through a typical day of family sparring, questionable business dealings, and forced conviviality with neighbors and associates. Underlying Babbitt's conformity, however, is a restless sense of the emptiness of his life, which grows more pronounced, and leads, as the novel progresses, to various attempts at escape—camping trips to the Maine woods, half-hearted efforts at romance, flirtations with leftist causes. When Babbitt's un-conventionality becomes noticeable to the "Good Citizen's League," an organization of his former associates designed to squash just the sort of troublesome independence that Babbitt is exhibiting, they bring pressure to bear on him and he eventually wilts. With the additional motivation of his wife's illness (which also offers him a face-saving means of returning to the fold), Babbitt abandons his rebellion and takes up his former existence a beaten man. From the perspective of this summary, *Babbitt* is a solid work of social realism, drawing much of its power for us as readers from its corroboration of our sense of how things are, or how they must be, for someone in Babbitt's shoes. *Babbitt* is more than "merely" realistic, but its success as a novel is anchored in its depiction of a real world of Floral Heights suburbia, of Ford automobiles, of dismal obligatory dinners, of realtors' conventions, and of the cash nexus that holds them all together.

When we think of social realism in the American novel, we generally think of those qualities set forth by William Dean Howells, the foremost theorist of American literary realism, in his 1891 collection of critical essays on the subject, *Criticism and Fiction.* We think of stories drawn from contemporary everyday life and familiar settings, of believable characters, such as those we ourselves might know and meet, people whose lives are, nonetheless, often touched, like our own, by complex and engrossing problems. We expect that the characters in such novels will speak in ordinary, everyday, colloquial English. We expect that there will be a good deal of dialogue, so that the characters themselves will reveal much of their own story. We expect the story to be told from a limited point of view, since in real life none of us, including the author or the narrator who is given the story to tell, can know everything. We expect that the author will remain well in the background, not obviously manipulating the action.

If we look closely at *Babbitt*, we find much that corresponds to these precepts of Howellsian realism. There is in *Babbitt* a full accounting and depiction of middle-American life in the 1920s. Mark Schorer lists the topics of the novel, and they provide a wide and thorough representation of Babbitt's milieu, including "Politics, Leisure, Club Life, Trade Association Conventions, Class Structure and Attitudes, Conventional Religion, 'Crank' Religion, Labor Relations, Marriage and the Family, and such lesser topics as The Barbershop and The Speakeasy" (Schorer 1961, 352). Each of the subjects is treated in remarkable detail. A typical passage of description suggests the full attention that Lewis, as realist, brings to the world of his novel. Here is Babbitt, driving to work in the morning:

> He admired each district along his familiar route to the office: The bungalows and shrubs and winding irregular driveways of Floral Heights. The one-story shops on Smith Street, a glare of plate-glass and new yellow brick; groceries and laundries and drug-stores to supply the more immediate needs of East side housewives. The market gardens in Dutch Hollow, their shanties patched with corrugated iron and stolen doors. Billboards with crimson goddesses nine feet tall advertising cinema films, pipe tobacco, and talcum powder. The old "mansions" along Ninth Street, S.E., like aged dandies in filthy linen; wooden castles turned into boarding-houses, with muddy walks and rusty hedges, jostled by fast-intruding garages, cheap apartment-houses, and fruit-stands conducted by bland, sleek Athenians. Across the belt of railroad tracks, factories with high-perched water-tanks and tall stacks—factories producing condensed milk, paper boxes, lighting-fixtures, motor cars. Then the business center, the thickening darting traffic, the crammed trolleys unloading, and high doorways of marble and polished granite. (28–29)

This is textbook realism, the catalogue of neighborhoods, buildings, and street-sights that the main character passes as he takes the familiar morning drive to his real-estate office. There is no apparent authorial plotting or selection here. With the exception of the reference to the "crimson goddesses" on the billboards, and the simile comparing the old mansions to "aged dandies in filthy linen," there is virtually no figurative language that might call attention to the author, or to the fact that he is, indeed, the creator of all this. The author is not overtly commenting here on the scene, or telling us what he thinks about it, or what we ought to think about it. He tells us only that Babbitt admired it all. Lewis gives us a close, visual rendering of "the system that works," and he gives it to us in a kind of writing that has been compared to a photograph.

Babbitt *and Realism*

If Lewis is often described as a notable photographer, he is also praised as a mimic, a realistic recorder of American speech sounds and patterns and rhythms of the sort that led H. L. Mencken—also a keen linguistic scholar—to a lifelong fascination with the individualities of American English, which he recorded in his book *The American Language* (1919–1948). Perhaps no American writer except Mark Twain had Lewis's ear for human speech. Take the snatches of overheard conversation in *Babbitt*, the "Say, jever hear the one . . ." of the dirty-joke-swapping salesmen in the smoking-car Pullman, or the perfunctory "snoway talkcher father" with which Mrs. Babbitt reprimands her children at the breakfast table. Take the oral record of typical morning inanities as George F. Babbitt attempts to implicate his wife in the agonizing daily decision of what to wear to work:

> "How about it? Shall I wear the brown suit another day?"
>
> "Well, it looks awfully nice on you."
>
> "I know, but gosh, it needs pressing."
>
> "That's so. Perhaps it does."
>
> "It certainly could stand being pressed, all right."
>
> "Yes, perhaps it wouldn't hurt it to be pressed."
>
> "But gee, the coat doesn't need pressing. No sense in having the whole darn suit pressed, when the coat doesn't need it."
>
> "That's so."
>
> "But the pants certainly need it, all right. Look at them—look at those wrinkles—the pants certainly do need pressing."
>
> "That's so. Oh, Georgie, why don't you wear the brown coat with the blue trousers we were wondering what we'd do with them?"
>
> "Good Lord! Did you ever in all my life know me to wear the coat of one suit and the pants of another? What do you think I am? A busted bookkeeper?"
>
> "Well, why don't you put on the dark gray suit to-day, and stop in at the tailor and leave the brown trousers?"
>
> "Well, they certainly need— Now where the devil is that gray suit?" (10–11)

Here, Lewis reveals not only his keen ear, but his skill in using everyday conversation as a revelation of relationships within a marriage. Babbitt, the self-styled man of decision and action, can't get himself dressed in the morning without his wife's help. He seeks Myra's advice on a mundane sartorial decision. She mirrors his uncertainty until, wearying of his indecisiveness, she offers a solution that he immediately and harshly ridicules. She responds with an acceptable decision that her husband follows, without acknowledgment, let alone thanks. End of incident. A typical bit of dialogue, realistically rendered. Yet the brief morning verbal exchange here reveals much about the Babbitts and their life together, the blustering but ineffectual husband and the bland and self-effacing, but indispensable wife, locked into their own version of the age-old battle of the sexes.

The novel has many such examples of human talk, set before us with uncanny accuracy. One verification of the enduring lifelike quality of the book's diction was revealed when actor Pat Hingle brought Babbitt back to life, forty-six years later, by delivering verbatim Babbitt's speech to the realtors, this time to an approving audience of the Duluth Lions' Club in April 1968.[9]

But the reader of Babbitt who is alert to the traditions and practices of literary realism in the American social novel soon discovers that there is an important sense in which Lewis characteristically diverges from realism's standards. That divergence is seen most clearly in his tone and his style. For if Lewis fills his best novels, like *Babbitt*, with the *material* of realism, he usually abandons a key *technique* of realism, the technique that calls for the author to adopt a low profile, be unobtrusive, and let the story and the characters appear to tell the tale themselves. What soon becomes evident in reading a book like *Babbitt* is that Lewis, or his characteristic narrative voice, is constantly and vociferously intruding into the description, the action, and even the dialogue, telling us, through various means, what he thinks of it all, and, by implication, what we should think of it all. As an example of this authorial intrusion, note the scene in which the Zenith Athletic Club, the luncheon oasis for Babbitt and his crowd, is described.

> The Zenith Athletic Club is not athletic and it isn't exactly a club, but it is Zenith in perfection. . . . It is the largest club in the city, and its chief hatred is the conservative Union Club, which all

sound members of the Athletic call "a rotten, snobbish, dull expensive old hole—not one Good Mixer in the place—you couldn't hire me to join." Statistics show that no member of the Athletic has ever refused election to the Union, and of those who are elected sixty-seven percent resign from the Athletic and are thereafter heard to say, in the drowsy sanctity of the Union lounge, "The Athletic would be a pretty good hotel, if it were more exclusive."

The Athletic Club building is nine stories high, yellow brick with glassy roof-garden above and portico of huge limestone columns below. The lobby, with its thick pillars of porous Caen stone, its pointed vaulting, and a brown glazed-tile floor like well-baked bread crust, is a combination of cathedral-crypt and rathskellar. The members rush into the lobby as though they were shopping and hadn't much time for it. Thus did Babbitt enter, and to the group standing by the cigar-counter he whooped, "How's the boys? How's the boys? Well, well, fine day!"(47)

There are several significant departures from realism in this passage. Note that the authorial voice alerts us, in the first sentence, to the hypocritical quality of the Zenith Athletic Club (neither athletic nor a club), but since hypocrisy is the norm in Zenith's social relationships, it is an indisputable emblem of Zenith itself. The hypocritical nature of the club members is then demonstrated in the next two sentences where we learn that their sour-grapes attitude toward the more exclusive Union Club is the expression of pure envy. The authorial voice is characterized by a mocking irony which, by means of some "statistics" (which we doubt ever existed except in the mind of the narrator), we as readers are invited to share. Indeed, given the breadth and vigor of the condemnation, we are *compelled* to share it. In this introduction, then, to Babbitt's club, Lewis has thrown down realist precepts and jumped on them. Although we may enjoy the results, he is telling us rather than showing us.

He does begin to show us in the second paragraph. The pictorial details here are certainly graphic and convincing. The reader easily visualizes the building and the lobby, and Babbitt's rapid entry into it. But the scene is more than a verbal reproduction. The mocking authorial presence is soon evident here as well, as is suggested in the yoking together of the incongruous images of cathedral-crypt and rathskellar, and in the implication of forced jollity and animation on the part of the businessmen as they enter. As the chapter continues, and Lewis warms to his task, the pretensions of the building's interior are more and more baldly revealed with its "somewhat musicianless musicians'-gallery, and tapestries believed to illustrate the granting of Magna Carta," and its huge stone fireplace "which the club's advertising-pamphlet asserted to be not only larger than any of the fireplaces in European castles but of a draught incomparably more scientific. It was also much cleaner, as no fire had ever been built in it" (50–51).

There is, of course, no way for the author to disappear completely, even in the most severely realistic work. As readers, we realize that a process of authorial selection and choice has gone on that has resulted in the characters and story before us. We understand that even the most apparently neutral, value-free language of a text encodes personal and cultural attitudes that can be isolated and held up for analysis. Indeed, there is no such thing as a literary work of pure realism. Pure realism would be the telephone book—and only the white pages at that. Every work of art is more than a mirror image or a tape recording. It is the evidence of a choosing, structuring, reflecting, meaning-making mind at work. But it is also clear, before one reads more than a page or two into any of his major novels, that Lewis, through his narrative voice, assumes a far more obvious presence in his novels than that voice we might find in a novel by Howells, Dreiser, Wharton, or Steinbeck.

In short, if Lewis is the great sociologist of literary mid-America, he is also the greatly antisocial sociologist of that territory and thus the title of realist does not quite fully encompass his methodology. To describe Lewis's presence in a novel like *Babbitt*, we need to examine the more problematic title Lewis is often assigned—that of satirist.

5

Satire and Style in *Babbitt*

Out of the incongruity between mundane circumstance and heroic
ideal, material fact and spiritual hunger, democratic middle-class
society and desire for cultural definition, theory of equality and fact
of social and economic inequality, the Declaration of Independence
and the Mann Act, the Gettysburg Address and the Gross National
Product, the Battle Hymn of the Republic and the Union Trust
Company, the Horatio Alger ideal and the New York Social Register—between what men would be and must be, as acted out in
American experience, has come much pathos, no small amount of
tragedy, and also a great deal of humor.
          —Louis D. Rubin, Jr., "The Great American Joke"[1]

The dynamics of our American life have tended to make humorists of
us, rather than satirists. Thus runs the common judgment of our country's cultural critics. Ambrose Bierce, "Bitter Bierce" as he was called—
who did his best in late nineteenth-century America to compensate for
the shortage of national bile—noted in his definition of "Satire" in his
Devil's Dictionary that "in this country satire never had more than a
sickly and uncertain existence, for the soul of it is wit, wherein we are
dolefully deficient, the humor that we mistake for it, like all humor,

being tolerant and sympathetic. Moreover, although Americans are endowed by their Creator with abundant vice and folly, it is not generally known that these are reprehensible qualities, wherefore the satirist is popularly regarded as a sour-spirited knave, and his every victim's outcry for codefendants evokes a national assent."[2]

Closer to our own times, Richard Bridgman has assessed at some length the national resistance to a biting and aggressive satire. Among the causes Bridgman cites for our preference for kindly humor over lashing satire are our lack of censorship and strongly fixed moral standards, the bewildering range of behavior tolerated in America, and the vaunted American sympathy for the underdog.[3] There is much to support Bridgman's assertions. Certainly there is no compelling requirement for witty satire if an outright and direct frontal attack is permitted by the society of the times. Why, except for the fun of it, go to the trouble of devising veiled and ironic insults when an open and abusive cussing-out of one's victim is permitted? Historically, satire has flourished in periods of official or unofficial censorship, when the sting of scorn has, to avoid detection and punishment, been concealed in what appears to be an approving bouquet.

Consider Herman Melville's avoidance of the strict religious censor of the 1840s in his early novel, *Typee*, as he describes from his firsthand experience as a youthful sailor, a South Seas island native celebration:

> Although I had been baffled in my attempt to learn the origin of the Feast of the Calabashes, yet it seemed very plain to me that it was principally, if not wholly, of a religious nature. As a religious solemnity, however, it had not at all corresponded with the horrible descriptions of Polynesian worship which we have received in some published narratives, and especially in those accounts of the evangelized islands with which the missionaries have favored us. Did not the sacred character of these persons render the purity of their intentions unquestionable, I should certainly be led to suppose that they had exaggerated the evils of Paganism, in order to enhance the merits of their own disinterested labors.[4]

Here, Melville's concealed attack on the missionaries was evasive enough to slide harmlessly by the moral censor. Unchallenged, *Typee*

was accepted by its readers—judging by the reviewers and the sales—
as a sunny tale of travel and adventure. Moreover, the perceptive and
sympathetic reader that Melville must have hoped for in such a passage
would have been privately delighted at the audacity of this masked
insult to the well-established forces of official piety.

By the time of Sinclair Lewis's great novels of the 1920s, the
battles against the most repressive forms of literary censorship in the
United States had been largely won. In the publishing history of Theodore Dreiser's *Sister Carrie* (1900) could be traced the struggle to tell
something of the truth about contemporary urban moral and economic
life. Lewis, like all those who followed Dreiser, benefited from the
freedoms that had been earned, however much these hard-won victo-
ries over the censor neutralized the satirist's need for creative indirection. Still, middle-class Americans were, as *Babbitt* was to show, yet
hostage to a series of clannish beliefs powerful enough to determine
their pleasures as well as their responsibilities. If Dreiser and Stephen
Crane and Frank Norris had lifted the lid from the lives of the American urban underclass, writers like Lewis—and Kate Chopin and Edith
Wharton before him—had shown that the middle and upper classes,
insulated by their money and position from the rawest forces of environmental determinism, could preserve a rigidity of judgment in their
own sphere, in which the moral censor and lockstep social standards
were still in control. As Lewis said of Babbitt: "Just as he was an Elk,
a Booster, and a member of the Chamber of Commerce, just as the
priests of the Presbyterian Church determined his every religious belief
and the senators who controlled the Republican Party decided in little
smoky rooms in Washington what he should think about disarma-
ment, tariff, and Germany, so did the large national advertisers fix the
surface of his life, fix what he believed to be his individuality" (80–81).
By the time of *Babbitt*, though, the system was headed for the sort of
breakdown that was forever to characterize the Roaring Twenties as
a time in which the old restraints were being cast off with increasing
frequency.

In this sense, Lewis came along at just the right moment. While
his *Main Street*, in 1920, had ended with a defeated Carol Kennicott
back in the town which had thwarted her fitful efforts at reform, the
revolt from the village was, with this literary coup de grace, essentially

over. Coming after Howells's *A Modern Instance* (1882), Harold Frederic's *The Damnation of Theron Ware* (1896), and Edgar Lee Masters's *Spoon River Anthology* (1915), *Main Street* had announced unequivocally and for all time that the American small town was not the unalloyed friendship village of our mythology.[5] As *Hamlet* had marked the end of the tradition of revenge tragedy in the Renaissance, so *Main Street* marked the end of the revolt-from-the-village tradition in American literature. As had Shakespeare's famous play, Lewis's novel had made clear that there was little more to be said on its subject. With the definitive last word provided by *Main Street*, you couldn't, after 1920, "keep 'em down on the farm," as village-born Babbitt was to prove in Lewis's next novel.

So if Babbitt and his Zenith clan are corralled within their narrow limits, they are, at the same time, surrounded and threatened by a bewildering array of alternative life-styles in the modern metropolis. This is depicted by various means in the novel, ranging from the rebellious behavior of Babbitt's own children, to the disquieting bohemianism of his neighbors, the Dopplebraus, to the descriptions of "the dozen contradictory Zeniths which together make up the true and complete Zenith" (174). Hence, Lewis's montage of vignettes, panning across the city, occurs at key moments in the novel. The technique serves to reveal myriad social and moral options from which the city's modern inhabitants might bravely choose; but, as in Babbitt's case, they rarely do. Thus, Lewis heightens the irony of the novel by revealing that the mind-forged manacles by which Babbitt is bound are as much the product of his own timid conformity as they are attributable to the controlling forces of the large culture. In both cases, though, *Babbitt's* phenomenal popular success, and its immediate impact on its readers was due in no small part to its depiction of the bankruptcy of the moral mythology with which middle-class and business life in America had been invested. Lewis was fortunate to have come on the scene just as the emperor's new clothes were disappearing.

At the same time that Lewis could, in the 1920s, attract enough liberal thinkers among the populace to guarantee him a wide readership, he was also fortunate, as a gadfly of the status quo, that the objects of his attack were still sufficiently powerful and entrenched to charge his work with the drama of genuine conflict. Like H. L. Mencken, Lewis neatly divided his audience into those who either cheered or were outraged by his writing. The resulting furor, from *Main Street* on, guaranteed him center stage. The incongruity between the American dream and the American reality that Louis D. Rubin, Jr., describes in the quotation beginning this chapter became the territory Sinclair Lewis claimed in fiction for his great novels of the 1920s. And to the pathos, tragedy, and humor that Rubin cites as the products of this incongruity, these Lewis novels would add another—satire.

If realism focuses on the way things are, satire operates in the considerable and lamentable gulf between how things are and how they should be. The realist in Lewis, as we have seen, had equipped him with a sharp eye and a keen ear for the actualities of American life. The satirist in Lewis, however, left him unsatisfied with rendering only an accurate visual and aural representation of this reality. For the satirist is always possessed of a discriminating moral sense, a perception of an ideal, which, although it may never be overtly present or even stated, nevertheless powerfully exists as the implied opposite of the stupidity and arrogance that is rampant in the world actually portrayed. The galling realization of how human subjects have fallen away from their rightful responsibilities and potentialities is what drives the satirist's pen. And since the object is to attack as effectively as possible the actual mischief ascendant in the world, the satirist employs the techniques and strategies of indirection as the means of this attack. The means of indirection—exaggeration, distortion, wit, irony, parody, and so forth—heighten the reader's sense of the incongruity between what is and what should be, and render delightful what might, in a plain and straightforward denunciation, be predictable and dull.

Mocking laughter is, as satire shows us, more than a defense against the insanity of much that surrounds us. The harsh laughter of satire is a kind of terrifying power that the satirist wields in exorcising our false gods. Once something presumptuous has been laughed at, it can never quite regain its hold over us. As Mark Twain's Philip Traum says in "The Mysterious Stranger," "Power, money, persuasion, supplication, persecution—these can lift at a colossal humbug—push it a little—weaken it a little, century by century; but only laughter can blow it to rags and atoms at a blast. Against the assault of laughter nothing can stand."[6]

The techniques and strategies of satire account for much of the form and style of *Babbitt*, for example, its tendency to move quickly from one topic to another, covering the entire range of middle-class business life in America, from its ugliest aspect—its racial, ethnic, and religious bigotry and its cutthroat commercial practices—to its essentially harmless, merely silly pursuits of diversion and pleasure. The effect is to suggest a world not so much of business as of busy-ness—a crowded scene in frantic motion, yet without any real move-ment toward specific and worthwhile goals. As a result, there is much emphasis on surfaces—names, household articles, colors, brands, lists, representations drawn from the popular media—and on distortion of these surfaces in order to heighten the sense of incongruity with the unnamed ideal.[7]

Satire in the form of an indirect attack on what is, from the moral standpoint of what ought to be, finds expression throughout *Babbitt*. On the most elementary level of sentence style and rhetoric, it may be seen in Lewis's constant juxtaposing of the sublime and the mundane. In the opening chapter, we find Babbitt asleep in the sleeping porch of his Floral Hills home, dreaming of his romantic "fairy child" who waited for him "in the darkness beyond mysterious groves. . . . She was so slim, so white, so eager! She cried that he was gay and valiant, that she would wait for him, that they would sail—

Rumble and bang of the milk-truck."(6)

The jarring effect here depends on the sardonic undercutting of Babbitt's romantic dream, rendered in a mellifluous and elevated dic-tion, by the harsh and ugly noises of the very real milk-truck.

On nearly every page where the authorial voice is telling or de-scribing, the reader finds this kind of ironic pairing. "To George F. Babbitt, as to most prosperous citizens of Zenith, his motor car was poetry and tragedy, love and heroism. The office was his pirate ship but the car his perilous excursion ashore" (23). Here, Lewis satirizes the American male's deification of his automobile by describing it in terms of high art and elevated emotion. The common-sense, realistic conception of the car, though unstated, is clearly present here. A car is a means of getting from one place to another, a conveyance, a device for transportation. But all of this is lost on Babbitt and his brethren, and the authorial voice mocks the triviality of their devotion to Detroit iron by raising it to an absurdly spiritual plane. As T. J. Matheson notes, Lewis give us "a kind of satiric fantasy world where spiritual terms, having been cut off completely from their original contexts, are misused as a matter of course, the words themselves having remained even though the states of being they once described have been forgotten" (Matheson, 39). Listen to the authorial voice commenting on the ideals of a group of traveling salesmen:

> To them, the Romantic Hero was no longer the knight, the wandering poet, the cowpuncher, the aviator, nor the brave young district attorney, but the great sales-manager, who had an Analysis of Merchandizing Problems on his glass-topped desk, whose title of nobility was "Go-getter," and who devoted himself and all his young samurai to the cosmic purpose of Selling—not of selling anything in particular, for or to anybody in particular, but pure Selling. (119)

Here, knightly ideals and romantic careers are yoked together with the ignoble practices of salesmanship. Lewis also establishes himself, here and elsewhere in his fiction, as perhaps the inventor—certainly the popularizer—of Ironic Capitalization. It is a device used frequently in *Babbitt* (Arising in the morning, Babbitt "put on the rest of his uniform as a Solid Citizen" [11]; or "Verona giggled, momentarily victor in the greatest of Great Wars, which is the family war" [20]; or, " 'I'll tell you Ted, we've got to have Vision—' " [72]). In this device, the romantic inflation and the satiric deflation are both neatly shorthanded into the typographical ploy.

The inflation-deflation pattern often occurs as a structural device, as well as a device of diction. In structural terms, Lewis is partial to a strategy that might be called "the closing kicker." Myra Babbitt, for example, is described in some detail in her matronliness. The authorial voice concludes that she was "a good woman, a kind woman, a diligent woman, but no one, save perhaps Tinka her ten-year-old, was at all interested in her or entirely aware that she was alive"(10). Similarly, a long passage of description of the Babbitts' house and furnishings is followed by this: "In fact there was but one thing wrong with the Babbitt house: It was not a home" (16). Or, recall the description of the huge fireplace at the Zenith Athletic Club, extolling its modern virtues and its superiority to those of European castles. The paean closes with "It was also much cleaner, as no fire had ever been built in it" (51). The strategy of the closing kicker, then, is to undercut, with a short but devastating final phrase, the credibility of all of the considerable and apparently reasonable and sensible prose that has led up to it.

Sometimes, the device of the closing kicker is put into the words of a speaker who rambles on and on, ending up, unwittingly, hoist on his own petard. Babbitt himself is more than once found in this absurd position, as in the revelation of his opinions on labor unions and industrial conditions:

> A good labor union is of value because it keeps out radical unions, which would destroy property. No one ought to be forced to belong to a union, however. All labor agitators who try to force men to join a union should be hanged. In fact, just between ourselves, there oughtn't to be any unions allowed at all; and as it's the best way of fighting the unions, every business man ought to belong to an employer's-association and to the Chamber of Commerce. In union there is strength. So any selfish hog who doesn't join the Chamber of Commerce ought to be forced to. (39)

Babbitt's literary friend, T. Cholmondeley (Chum) Frink, who makes his living writing doggerel poems for the newspapers, is another character who falls victim to the closing kicker of Lewis's satire. This occurs at several points in the novel, first at the Babbitts' cocktail party, where Chum's earnest and enthusiastic pursuit—in private—of Babbitt's liquor is undercut by the narrator's presentation of Chum's saccharine public verses on the virtues of sobriety. Later in the book, Frink boozily confesses to having failed his poetic gifts for the easy dollars of a newspaper rhymer. But the extent of his bardic ambitions (" 'Know what I could've been? I could've been a Gene Field or a

James Whitcomb Riley. Maybe a Stevenson. I could've.' " [220]), is revealed in the distinctly minor-league status of his admired models. Thus, Chum stands before us, by his own admission, as hopelessly banal, not only in his performances, but even in his aspirations.

Lewis has an endless array of clever rhetorical variations for the closing kicker. In chapter 7, he details Babbitt's evening at home in a structurally brilliant variation of the inflation-deflation pattern that encompasses the entire chapter. It opens with a realistic description of Babbitt's living room and the mundane conversation between George and Myra, prior to bedtime. (" 'An apple a day keeps the doctor away,' he enlightened Mrs. Babbitt, for quite the first time in fourteen hours" [78]). In the next section, George takes his evening bath, and plays, contented and childish, in the bathwater, "a plump, smooth, pink, baldish, podgy goodman, robbed of the importance of spectacles, squatting in breast-high water. . . ." (80) Then out of the bath, and into his carefully prepared bed on his sleeping-porch, where he drops off to sleep. This is followed by a series of Lewis's cross-cutting scenes, a group of parallel vignettes of life across the spectrum of Zenith's social register, each beginning with the words "At that moment."

> At that moment in the city of Zenith, Horace Updike was making love to Lucile McKelvey in her mauve drawing-room on Royal Ridge, after their return from a lecture by an eminent English novelist.
>
> . . . .
>
> And at that moment in Zenith, a cocaine-runner and a prostitute were drinking cocktails in Healey Hanson's saloon on Front Street. [This followed by the man's shooting of the woman.]
>
> At that moment in Zenith, two men sat in a laboratory. For thirty-seven hours now they had been working on a report of their investigations of synthetic rubber.
>
> At that moment in Zenith, there was a conference of four union officials as to whether the twelve thousand coal miners within a hundred miles of the city should strike. . . .
>
> . . . .
>
> At that moment the steel and cement town which composed the factory of the Pullman Tractor Company of Zenith was running on night shift to fill an order of tractors for the Polish army.

. . . .

At that moment Seneca Doane, the radical lawyer, and Dr. Kurt Yavitch, the histologist (whose report of the destruction of epithelial cells under radium had made the name of Zenith known in Munich, Prague, and Rome), were talking in Doane's library.

. . . .

At that moment Lloyd Mallam, the poet, owner of the Hafiz Book Shop, was finishing a rondeau to show how diverting was life amid the feuds of medieval Florence, but how dull it was in so obvious a place as Zenith.

And at that moment George F. Babbitt turned ponderously in bed. . . .

Instantly he was in the magic dream. He was somewhere among unknown people who laughed at him. He slipped away, ran down the paths of a midnight garden, and at the gate the fairy child was waiting. Her dear and tranquil hand caressed his cheek. He was gallant and wise and well-beloved; warm ivory were her arms; and beyond perilous moors the brave sea glittered. (81–86)

The chapter is thus organized to enclose the excitement and variety of modern city life within the structural bookends comprised by the exceedingly dull evening of solid-citizen Babbitt. But whereas the chapter begins with Babbitt's unromantic waking existence, it closes with his dream life, a little whirl of romance and peril. Lewis even shifts the style into high romance, with the polysyndeton repetition of connectors ("gallant and wise and well-beloved") and the reversal of word order ("warm ivory were her arms"). After the strong and detailed realistic language of the remainder of the chapter, this closing kicker completes the chapter's reversal of Lewis's usual stylistic pattern— inflation undercut by deflation—to the opposite. At the same time, from the standpoint of content and meaning, Babbitt's comfortable life, cushioned from the shocks and significance of the real, consequential world (as revealed in the cross-cutting scenes), is rendered even more trivial as he escapes into his dream fantasy at the end.

Lewis has still more varied techniques for his closing kicker. He sometimes bunches together a tight series of them, Gatling-gun style: "But Babbitt was virtuous. He advocated, though he did not practice, the prohibition of alcohol; he praised, though he did not obey, the laws against motor-speeding; he paid his debts; he contributed to the church, the Red Cross, and the Y.M.C.A.; he followed the custom of his clan and cheated only as it was sanctified by precedent" (40). Similarly, Lewis provides a paragraph of Babbitt's address to the Zenith Boosters' Club that is full of noble sentiments about the need of the realtor to know his city in all its faults and virtues, and then follows this with a paragraph detailing, on one subject after another, what Babbitt does—and doesn't—know about Zenith: "Though he did know the market price, inch by inch, of certain districts of Zenith, he did not know whether the police force was too large or too small, or whether it was in alliance with gambling and prostitution. He knew . . . but he did not know . . ." (38–39). The pattern continues, with the "not know's" quickly overwhelming the "know's," leaving us with a series of closing kickers that kick the notion of the Visionary Realtor unceremoniously downstairs.

Lewis underscores Babbitt's occupational ineptitude with yet another version of the closing kicker when we see Babbitt at his office, attempting to dictate a letter to his secretary. His efforts are so fumbling and garbled as to be incoherent to all but the coolly efficient Miss McGoun. Back at her desk, she translates his feeble directive into a forceful and effective letter for which Babbitt, of course, takes full credit when it is placed before him for his signature (31–32).

Sometimes, the closing kicker is used so heavy-handedly that the reader refuses to give it credence. Such is the response of several critics and numerous readers to the paired dinner scenes in chapter 15 of the novel. The Babbitts, wishing to rise socially, invite the upper-crust McKelveys to dinner, and the McKelveys reluctantly accept. Obviously bored, the McKelveys go home at 9:45 on the excuse of Mrs. McKelvey's "headache." The Babbitts are plunged into despair, but still hope for a return invitation. When none is forthcoming, the Babbitts find their social aspirations dashed. Immediately following this episode, the Babbitts repeat the process, this time in the position of the McKelveys, in accepting a dinner invitation to the home of the Overbrooks, a failed insurance salesman and his threadbare wife. Unwittingly, the Babbitts follow, step by step, the behavior of the McKelveys, right down to the early departure and the decision that a return invitation would only repeat the agony and make the Overbrooks feel out of place. It is all too contrived to be believable, a case where the satiric device falls prey to a too-obvious depiction of Zenith's social pecking-order. A similar example of overkill may be found in chapter 8, when Babbitt and his friends deride the conversational limitations of small-town folks. Their jeering put-down, of course, features the same sort of repetitiousness that they complain of in their rural counterparts.

The closing kicker, exemplified so frequently in sentence-, paragraph-, and chapter-level forms, is also employed in the larger structure of the novel. As the story progresses, Babbitt is depicted as growing increasingly restive under the bonds of conformity. Finally, he rebels and attempts to fashion an individual life for himself. But his personal resolve is too weak to withstand the external pressures brought to bear on him by his conformist acquaintances and he finds himself forced back into his old rut. As he confides, finally, to his son Ted, " 'I don't know's I've accomplished anything except just get along. I figure out I've made about a quarter of an inch out of a hundred possible rods' "(319). The ultimate closing kicker is Babbitt's fate itself, an ironic recognition that all his yearnings and aspirations and attempts to escape have gone for naught. A conclusion in which nothing is concluded.

Lewis's talent for mimicry, noted in chapter 4 as one of the great strengths of his realism, is often applied to satiric ends in *Babbitt*'s many versions of parody. Parody involves exaggeration of the characteristic style and manner of an author or speaker or particular kind of discourse. The trick of parody is, first of all, to choose as the target a style that is already nearly pretentious, close to the edge of self-consciousness or affectation. Then, by simply overemphasizing, over-doing, the stylistic affectation, the parodist pushes the targeted style over the brink, where it falls into absurdity. Often parody involves choosing a subject that is ludicrously inappropriate to the original target, and to the seriousness with which that original is treated. Such is the case with E. B. White's famous parody of Hemingway's *Across the River and into the Trees* (1950). In the parody, "Across the Street and into the Grill," White ridicules the heavy-handed postbattle pontificating of Hemingway's Colonel Cantwell by reducing the original

Good Gray Warrior to a meek little office manager, who nevertheless treats with deadly Hemingway seriousness the stains on his fingers from a balky mimeograph machine, and the details accompanying taking his secretary to lunch.[8]

In *Babbitt*, however, Lewis seldom finds it necessary or appropriate to range into this realm of wide discrepancy, since it might call into question the general air of reality in the work. There is little need for Lewis to look beyond Babbitt's immediate environment for his parodic purposes, since the targets that already exist there are quite adequate to the satirist's needs. So, Lewis parodies those aspects of Babbitt's world—especially the mass media and its practitioners—that are nearly ridiculous as a type to start with, and that require only a few deft strokes from the author to be rendered laughable. Such are the newspaper and magazine self-help ads for correspondence courses that Babbitt's impressionable teenage son Ted shows to his parents as his hoped-for alternative to further public schooling:

> He snatched from the back of his geometry half a hundred advertisements of those home-study courses which the energy and foresight of American commerce have contributed to the science of education. The first displayed the portrait of a young man with a pure brow, an iron jaw, silk socks, and hair like patent leather. Standing with one hand in his trousers-pocket and the other extended with chiding forefinger, he was bewitching an audience of men with gray beards, paunches, bald heads, and every other sign of wisdom and prosperity. Above the picture was an inspiring educational symbol—no antiquated lamp or torch or owl of Minerva, but a row of dollar signs. The text ran: (65)

What follows in the novel's pages is an actual reproduction of a display advertisement, complete with boxed, highlighted features, varied type faces and sizes, and embellishing dollar-signs. The main text of the advertisement is the familiar rags-to-riches narrative of a shy nonentity of a shipping clerk—just the sort of reader to whom the appeal is directed—who, with the aid of Professor Peet's Course in Public Speaking, is now on the road to "Prosperity and Domination," as represented by a twelve-cylinder automobile, a place in high society, and a private-school education for his children. All this under the step-by-step guid- ·

ance of the charismatic Professor W. F. Peet, "graduate of some of our leading universities," and holder of the secrets of a masterful personality, which are, of course, available to the novitiate who has the price of the course.

Like all satire, this parody exists in relationship to its opposite, whether stated or unstated. Here, Professor Peet's mailing address unwittingly tells the only truth in the ad: "Shortcut Educational Pub. Co., Sandpit, Iowa." Ted seeks the easy shortcut to an education, a royal road to success and power. But Professor Peet's siren appeal is a fraud and a delusion, as is suggested by the sage's nowhere address, whose gritty connotations bespeak a failed venture and serve to effectively undercut the wheezingly upbeat rhetoric of the rest of the ad.

Lewis continues the satire on false paths to self-improvement with Ted's later enthusiasm for a boxing and self-defense course by mail. Once again, Lewis produces the ad verbatim, and once again it is a parody that requires but little exaggeration of what might have been the model. This ad strikes a familiar chord. Many of Lewis's later readers will recall what might have been the original, which graced the back cover of countless comic books in the early and midtwentieth century. It featured a skinny young man at the beach, who has sand kicked in his face by a jeering bully. Back in his own room, the undernourished young man kicks a chair in frustrated retaliation and resolves to send for the advertised course in bodybuilding. A short time later, and under the influence of some mysterious process called "dynamic tension," he appears again at the beach, this time as a smoothly muscled and self-confident he-man, who quickly dispatches the offending bully, before a group of admiring females.

The parodies continue as Ted jumps to the appeal of becoming an "Osteo-vitalic Physician." ("Money! Money! Money!!" screams the ad), or of earning a cool ten dollars a day teaching the "Hindu System of Vibratory Breathing and Mental Control," or of becoming and adventuresome, well-paid, and far-traveled "Finger-Print Detective." By this time, the flush of instant success has overwhelmed Babbitt's original skepticism, and he and Ted share the heady and rarified air of these educational pipe dreams, as together they pore over the notices and ads from mail box universities, teaching "Short-story Writing and Improving the Memory, Motion-picture acting and Developing the Soul-power," and so on (70–71). Once again, however, it is the normally acquiescent and opinionless Mrs. Babbitt who punctures the bubble of speculation by announcing, " 'I think those correspondence-courses are terrible!' " Aghast, Babbitt pronounces her opposition to be nonsense. But he is gradually brought back to earth by her quite legitimate objections, and finally announces to Ted that an actual college education is still the surest way to wealth, and that a real bachelor of arts commands more respect than " 'the degree of Stamp-licker from the Bezuzus Mail-order University' " (73). Thus, prestige and profits, Babbitt's strongest justifications for attending a real college, win out at last over the fraudulent mail-order pedagogues. The parodies of get-rich-quick correspondence courses are thus exceeded in their satiric effect by Babbitt's final argument that Ted should go to a real university, ironically, for all the wrong reasons.

Parodies of advertising also appear in *Babbitt* as satiric examples of the substitution of bogus art for genuine art in a commercialized America. For Chum Frink, Babbitt's high priest of the literary mysteries, the ads for Prince Albert pipe tobacco and Zeeco automobiles, duly presented in the text, along with Chum's learned annotations on their various rhetorical and stylistic beauties, are "the poetry of industrialism," opening up new fields of literary endeavor for aspiring bards of commerce (100–101).

The sublime heights of Chum Frink's own lyrical outpourings and the ads that he treasures for their classy appeal are followed later in the novel by the deliciously low ad for a burlesque show. Babbitt and his pub-crawling friends, cutting loose at the realtors' convention in the city of Monarch—where their inhibitions have fallen away in direct proportion to the number of miles that separate them from the familiar strictures of Zenith—are easy victims for the immoralities hinted at behind the ad's blizzard of slang and sleaze:

Old Colony Theater

Shake the Old Dogs to the
WROLLICKING WRENS
The bonniest bevy of beauteous

bathing babes in burlesque.
Pete Menutti and his
Oh, Gee, Kids.

This is the straight steer, Benny, the painless chicklets of the Wrol-licking Wrens are the cuddlingest bunch that ever hit town. Steer the feet, get the card board, and twist the pupils to the PDQest show ever. You will get 111% on your kale in this fun-fest. The Calroza Sisters are sure some lookers and will give you a run for your gelt. Jock Silbersteen is one of the pepper lads and slips you a dose of real laughter. Shoot the up and down to Jackson and West for graceful tappers. . . . Something doing, boys. Listen to what the Hep Bird twitters. (143)

The ad is later unmasked in all its fraudulent exaggerations and forced hyperbole, as the cigar-smoking and slightly drunk Babbitt and his friends watch at the burlesque show "while a chorus of twenty daubed, worried, and inextinguishably respectable grandams swung their legs in the more elementary chorus-evolutions, and a Jewish comedian made vicious fun of Jews" (143–44). Lewis thus steps in to deflate the ad in his own hard terms.

Parodies of all sorts, of newspaper society columns and church news, of college alumni dinner announcements, of civic songs, are before us frequently in *Babbitt,* and serve, along with the more direct manifestations of Lewis's attack, as evidence of the densely packed disorder of Babbitt's world and its power to threaten and nearly over-whelm the sanitive and corrective function of the satirist.

Perhaps the most sustained and notable subject for parody in *Babbitt* is public oratory itself. As Mark Schorer reminds us, "Elocu-tion is an old American institution, and a windy, mindless rhetoric has been of its essence. Lewis's use of elocution adds a swelling note to the already loud *blat-blat* of that public voice that roars and clacks throughout the novels, and if Lewis lets Babbitt admire Chan Mott because he 'can make a good talk even if he hasn't got a doggone thing to say,' he is also making an observation on the empty and noisy restlessness of American life" (Schorer 1961, 353). Indeed, Babbitt makes his bid for local fame in his speech to the Zenith Real Estate Board, where he is the substitute speaker for the indisposed Chan Mott, and proves that Mott is not the only one who can please an audience without actually having anything to say. Babbitt's speech is reproduced in all its smug satisfaction and self-serving narrow-mindedness: " 'Here's the new generation of Americans: fellows with hair on their chests and smiles in their eyes and adding machines in their offices. We're not doing any boasting, but we like ourselves first-rate, and if you don't like us, look out—better get under cover before the cyclone hits town' " (151). With Babbitt's inane boosting of Zenith's commercial culture and his ominous, jowl-shaking warnings against the "liberals" ("irresponsible teachers and professors constitute the worst of this whole gang, and I am ashamed to say that several of them are on the faculty of our great State University!" [154]), he establishes himself as a new Demosthenes of snap, sales, and hundred percent Americanism, and finds himself making the rounds on the Zenith after-dinner speakers' circuit. Ironically, it is Babbitt's rise as an orator that marks his moral decline. Vergil Gunch praises Babbitt as a public speaker (" 'All this guff ought to bring a lot of business into your office. Good work! Keep it up!' " [155]). But this is the same Gunch who later maliciously and relentlessly forces a rebellious Babbitt back into submission, and we realize that Gunch's praise of Babbitt here is the equivalent of an ethical indictment. Furthermore, Gunch's cynical reference to Babbitt's rhetorical prowess (" 'all this guff' ") is an admission of the decline of the once-honorable tradition of American public oratory into a device for suppressing dissent and ensuring that the corrupt practices through which Gunch prospers will go on as usual.

Parodies of religious oratory are, like those of the business world, frequently put before us in Babbitt. Beginning with Mike Monday's viciously anti-intellectual assault on his spiritual detractors, Lewis presents us with an array of religious representatives in the novel whose speeches form an important part of his satire. Mike Monday (a thinly disguised parody of real-life ballplayer-turned-evangelist Billy Sunday) is an ex-prize-fighter who has taken to preaching, and who cuts loose in a stunning outburst of degraded oratory and invective:

> There's a lot of smart college professors and tea-guzzling slobs
> in this burg that say I'm a roughneck and a never-wuzzer and
> my knowledge of history is not-yet. Oh, there's a gang of woolly-

whiskered book-lice that think they know more than Almighty God, and prefer a lot of Hun science and smutty German criticism to the straight and simple Word of God. Oh, there's a swell bunch of Lizzie boys and lemon-suckers and pie-faces and infidels and beer-bloated scribblers that love to fire off their filthy mouths and yip that Mike Monday is vulgar and full of mush. Those pups are saying now that I hog the gospel-show, that I'm in it for the coin. Well, now listen, folks! I'm going to give those birds a chance! They can stand right up here and tell me to my face that I'm a galoot and a liar and a hick! Only if they do—if they do!—don't faint with surprise if some of those rum-dumm liars get one good swift poke from Mike, with all the kick of God's Flaming Righteousness behind the wallop! Well, come one, folks! Who says it? Who says Mike Monday is a four-flush and a yahoo? Huh? Don't I see anybody standing up? Well, there you are! Now I guess the folks in this man's town will quit listening to all this kyoodling from behind the fence; I guess you'll quit listening to the guys that pan and roast and kick and beef, and vomit out filthy atheism; and all of you'll come in, with every grain of pep and reverence you got, and boost all together for Jesus Christ and his everlasting mercy and tenderness! (83–84)

Monday's blast of vitriol is a satirical tour-de-force for Lewis. In one paragraph the author allows a bullying demagogue to both reveal and manipulate the simmering class hatred and resentment of those left behind by the march of history and intellect. Many of the devices of a national elocutionary tradition that has been debased almost beyond recognition are present here. By the end of the first few sentences, Monday has effectively polarized the situation: a plain, rough-speaking but God-fearing commoner who challenges the pretentious professors and intellectuals (suspiciously bearded, at that) and other effete types who dare to spurn the literal Holy Writ. The conflict is restated in parallel semantic and grammatical structure through the first three sentences, with Mike's gorge rising all the while, along with the level of invective. Yet Lewis the satirist is also present here, ensuring that we as readers do not miss the self-reflexive irony of Mike's foul-mouthed indictment of those " 'beer-bloated scribblers that love to fire off their filthy mouths,' " and his outrage at those who would dare to call him " 'vulgar.' "

Mike Monday's opening oratorical triad is followed by a statement that his detractors accuse him of pursuing gospel evangelism for the profits—a charge that, interestingly enough, he does not quite deny. Instead, he calls on his overeducated and cowardly tormentors to repeat the charges right here and now, to his face, for which he will give them a blow with " 'all the kick of God's flaming righteousness behind it.' " Having shifted the question of the honesty of his motives over into an arena where his pugilistic attainments might serve him better than reason and evidence, Mike crows forth his challenge to an audience which, we may assume, is notably devoid of college professors and Hun scientists. After another oratorical triad of repeated question, Mike sees no takers and can, by the inescapable logic he has just demonstrated, proclaim himself victorious over his despised detractors. Lewis brings Mike's abusive blast to a wonderfully incongruous conclusion by his sudden shift from foul invective to intoned praise " 'for Jesus Christ and his everlasting mercy and tenderness!' " The obligatory benediction invoking Christ's tender mercies comes here like the counterpunch of Mike's earlier career in the ring: an instinctive response to a stimulus—in this case the tabernacle setting and the fact that he is, after all, ending a sermon of sorts, and is expected to make at least a token reference to the virtues of Christian brotherhood and love.

After skewering the lowbrow proponents of religion, Lewis moves up the socioeconomic ladder to parody the middlebrow message of Mike Monday's more respectable suburban counterpart, and Babbitt's spiritual adviser, the Reverend John Dennison Drew, whose sonorous and impeccably WASP, three-named appellation itself announces his superiority to the vulgarly familiar Mike. But when Reverend Drew warbles his own brand of spiritual sustenance to Babbitt and his neighbors in the Chatham Road Presbyterian Church on a Sunday morning in December, his words betray him as effectively as did those of Mike Monday before his audience of the unwashed. Reverend Drew's sermons, we are told, are prized for their "intellectual quality," of which Lewis gives us a representative sample:

> "At this abundant harvest-time of the year," Dr. Drew chanted, "when, though stormy the sky and laborious the path to the drudging wayfarer, yet the hovering and bodiless spirit swoops back o'er

all the labors and desires of the past twelve months, oh, then it seems to me there sounds behind all our apparent failures the golden chorus of greeting from those passed happily on; and lo! on the dim horizon we see behind dolorous clouds the mighty mass of mountains—mountains of melody, mountains of mirth, mountains of might! (168–69)

Here is a parody of the vacuous spiritual optimism that soothes Babbitt and his class, an outpouring of treacle that possesses not even a shadow of an idea. Reverend Drew reveals himself as the Doctor Feelgood of the proper burghers of Zenith, and his message is a comfortable, stroking assurance that they need not be disturbed about the state of their souls. In a style heavy in high-toned, Tennysonian diction (" 'o'er,' " " 'lo!' ") and in marshmallow mountains of mellifluous alliteration, Reverend Drew manages to say absolutely nothing. Compared to his tissuey string of euphemisms, the harangue of Mike Monday is a veritable fount of information. Yet at the end of Dr. Drew's service, Babbitt meditates soberly on what he imagines are its profundities.

Lewis concludes his parody of contemporary religionists late in the novel, when Babbitt, with his wife, attends a "New Thought" meeting at which Mrs. Opal Emerson Mudge lifts the veils of mystery to reveal still another spiritual realm to Babbitt and his clan:

There are those who have seen the rim and outer seeming of the Logos there are those who have glimpsed and in enthusiasm possessed themselves of some segment of the Logos there are those who thus flicked but not penetrated and radioactivated by the Dynamis go always to and fro assertative that they possess and are possessed of the Logos and the Metaphysikos but this word I bring you this concept I enlarge that those that are not utter are not even inceptive and that holiness is in its definitive essence always always always whole-iness and—(286)

After an hour and seven minutes of this relentless, commaless flow, the Babbitts are mesemerized into submission, though both are hard put, later, to assign a specific meaning to this message from the Mudgean interior. George and Myra's attempt to unravel Mrs.

Mudge's Higher Thought, without even the benefits of punctuation to aid them, soon degenerates into an argument over George's extra-spiritual behavior. The point seems clear here, as in all the preceding depictions of religion in the novel. The church, in all its myriad—and fragmented—forms, has ceased to be a significant force in the lives of modern urbanites in America. Religion has fallen from relevance. When Lewis turns religion over to the crackpots, and when he lets them talk and talk and talk, we delight in its awful realness. But we also see, in the startling emptiness of their self-revelations, that they have nothing to offer for the correction of Babbitt's spiritual malaise, nor that of America as a whole. In the three spokespersons for religion in the novel, we find a portent of the vast and clacking spiritual void that Lewis will later present more fully in *Elmer Gantry*.

The satirist, it has been claimed, writes out of a sense of violated moral standards. It is easy, as Mark Schorer points out, to name these moral standards and values "that would save Zenith and Babbitt with it; they are love and friendship; kindness, tolerance, justice and integrity; beauty; intellect" (Schorer 1961, 355). But the satirist also realizes that the moralist's desire to pound the offenders to rags and pulp with a club is much less likely to move an audience than is the poisoned dart of wit and irony and parody. If, as Schorer claims, there is present in *Babbitt* little evidence of the positive virtues, we may attribute this to the indirection by which satire works.

Yet it is also true that we feel the presence of the redeeming virtues even when they are unstated, just because their perversions are paraded so insistently before us. Indeed, these perversions may threaten to overwhelm us, and leave us desperately grasping for something solid to hold on to. And not only do we as readers grasp for the saving values, so does the novel's central figure. If Babbitt's world, in its multitudinous disorder and its smug pursuit of pleasure and profits, seems impervious to the the moral thrust of satire, Babbitt himself is no such fortress of complacency. As committed as Lewis is to the techniques of realism and satire in *Babbitt*, he provides another facet to his main character that acts in opposition to the literal and the derisive, and to the surfaces on which they play. For there is also an interior Babbitt in the novel, a Babbitt of private dreams and unacknowledged hopes, who does not live by bread and business alone.

6

Impossible Dreams: *Babbitt* and Romance

Babbitt is a great novel of satiric realism not because it reproduces, unexamined, popular conceptions about an American type—the businessman. It is a major work because it looks beneath the assumed surface to reveal the individualities of the type, the way Babbitt diverges—in his secret dreams and longings—from the easy and unexamined generalizations.

If Lewis is a satirist, he has the satirist's keen moral sense of a better world than that which lies before him. If Lewis is a realist, he is also enough of a realist to recognize that, for all of the narrowness, the conformity, the smug self-satisfaction of his middle Americans, there is a lonely strain of romantic idealism within them that marks them as human and typical. As Sanford E. Marovitz has said, in describing the characteristic ambivalence of Lewis's characters, he writes of people as they actually are:

> Human beings generally are idealists and pragmatists; they are heroic in their daydreams and their bluster, but anxiety over their real state is the instigator of both. They shout for individualism more loudly as their support increases from conformists around them

who are shouting identical words. They yearn to be in the crowd without being of it, yet none are truly comfortable either way. They want domestic peace with fame and fortune. They want the limelight, yet they fear it, sometimes even shun it, then dream of what glory it might have brought. They find it easier to be honest with others than with themselves. And they struggle to maintain a good image though they may despise themselves at times for doing so; worse still, often they do not even recognize the hypocrisy underlying this internal conflict.[1]

Lewis's realist predecessors like Mark Twain, William Dean Howells, Frank Norris, Theodore Dreiser, and Edith Wharton all recognized the appeal to the hungering imagination for something more than life offered. This resistance to realism, this counter to the way things are, frequently finds expression in their fiction. In fact, it is fair to say that they were all stricter realists in theory than in practice. And at the same time that realistic criticism and literature was making its greatest advances, the popular press was awash in sentimental and formulaic romance, historical swashbucklers, costume dramas full of larger-than-life heroes and heroines and wild and improbable scenes and actions. Though the critics were harsh on these prodigies and fables, the public loved them, as they did in Shakespeare's days and as they do today. In this widespread and seemingly perverse fascination with the fiction of wishes, lies, and dreams, with the appeals of hope over experience, with the attractions of unreality, both serious and formulaic writers acknowledged a chronic human need. The great outpouring of Utopian novels at the end of the nineteenth century, including the Altrurian novels of the foremost realism theorist of the times, William Dean Howells, were further testimony to that need.

Sinclair Lewis's readers and critics have long been aware of this odd doubleness in his work and personality. When Sherwood Anderson described Lewis in 1922 as "a man writing who, wanting passionately to love the life about him, cannot bring himself to do so," he expressed what has become a characteristic judgment.[2] Perhaps no American writer of modern times has so insistently presented an ambivalent and divided artistic self to his public as has Lewis. Participant and enthusiast as well as observer and critic, the scourge of American villages, doctors, preachers, and businessmen, as well as—so Lewis later assured us—their heartiest well-wisher, Lewis remains a compelling cultural figure in our culture. It will be recalled that T. K. Whipple, in his essay on Lewis in *Spokesmen* over sixty years ago, concluded early in the writer's career that "Lewis is the most successful critic of American society because he is the best proof that his charges are just" (Whipple 1928, 228). And more recently, Mark Schorer, Sheldon Grebstein, D. J. Dooley, and Martin Light, in their books on Lewis, all argue convincingly that he was a writer possessed of eternally warring qualities. They find that on almost any level of personal or artistic performance Lewis presented a continuing split in sensibility: lonely introvert versus mad exhibitionist, coy romancer versus satiric realist, defender versus derider of intellect and art, alternately ridden by, and rejecting, material success. From this welter of contrarieties emerges what Schorer calls "the real enigma of his novels, a persistent conflict of values that clashed no less within him" (Schorer 1961, 4).

In this conflict of values it is Lewis the acid-tongued realist, the tormentor of Babbittry and middle America, who has received the most attention. "The fact is," one typical judgment runs, "that Lewis is dull when being positive, but delightful when being negative."[3] Yet in attempting to understand more clearly the paradox that Schorer and others have noted, and in trying to come to terms with George F. Babbitt and his society, we are driven back to a fuller consideration of the other Lewis, who would seem to have a place in the main current of American idealism, who with Emerson and Whitman would project on a native Midwestern landscape the values of democratic individualism and a sublime conception of the future. This is the Lewis who would present in his fiction idealized alternatives to the society whose chronicler he was; the Lewis who scored the "contradiction between pioneering myth and actual slackness" in America, and who wrote of himself that he "mocked the cruder manifestations of Yankee Imperialism because he was, at heart, a fanatic American."[4] This is the Lewis who in 1938 called Willa Cather the greatest living American novelist because "no other has so preserved our frontier . . . yet no one has more lucidly traced the post-pioneer American than she."[5]

These counterforces of affirmation are strongly present in *Babbitt*, and indeed in the body of all of his novels. Lewis's romantic idealism reveals itself in a pattern of affirmation composed of three recurring themes: the celebration of nature, the summoning-up of the visionary western future (objectified in architectural terms as the modern city), and the questing individual—always a native Midwesterner—who stands as harbinger or potential creator of this future.

To begin with Lewis's treatment of nature and landscape, it may be noted that, in *Babbitt* and elsewhere, Lewis's depictions of nature often seem flat and undeveloped, for all that he insists on its importance. Despite his claim that *Walden* was the chief influence on his formative years, and his high praise for Thoreau, Lewis's version of pastoral is often, unlike Thoreau's, merely the sentimental rapture of the urbanite in the countryside that has always flourished in our popular literature.[6] Nature in many of his novels, including *Babbitt*, is primarily a simple escape, intended to be restorative and beneficial. The urbanite who is ennobled and revivified by an interlude in Arcadia is a stock figure for Lewis. The milquetoast, citified hero of his early novel, *Our Mr. Wrenn* (1914), is, for example, propelled into self-reliance partly as a result of his walking trip through the English countryside. Similarly, in *The Innocents* (1917) an elderly New York couple set out on a walking trip across the country, and en route are rather incredibly transformed from shy nonentities into aggressive and successful go-getters.[7] City girls like Ruth Winslow of *The Trail of the Hawk* (1915) and Claire Boltwood of *Free Air* (1919) change—through contact with nature—from eastern, or "indoor" women, to western, or "outdoor" women, thus completing a required rite of passage for Lewis heroines. As Lewis's sympathetic treatment of them prepares us for his later favorable view of "outdoor" women like Carol Kennicott in *Main Street*, Edith Cortright in *Dodsworth*, and Ann Vickers in the novel of that name, so Lewis's dismissal of the "indoor" Gertie Cowles of *The Trail of the Hawk* anticipates his later unsympathetic treatment of "indoor" women like Myra Babbitt and Tanis Judique in *Babbitt*, Joyce Lanyon of *Arrowsmith*, and Fran Dodsworth in *Dodsworth*. Significantly, there are no "outdoor" women in *Babbitt*, and thus no women capable of accompanying or leading Babbitt out of his urban dilemma.

Alert to the worst excesses of sentimental pastoral, Lewis tempers his treatment of nature by including realistic and satiric details, as he does in the Maine woods scenes in *Babbitt*. In *The Job* (1917) a country-caused euphoria mistakenly brings Una Golden under the spell of "the thwarted boyish soul that persisted in Mr. Schwirtz's barbered, unexercised, coffee-soaked, tobacco-filled, whiskey-rotted, fattily-degenerated city body."[8] In *The Trail of the Hawk* Lewis at one point spoofs the clichés of popular wilderness fiction of the period, at the same time that he repeats its basic values:

> "If this were a story," said Carl, knocking the crusted snow from dead branches and dragging them toward the center of a small clearing, "the young hero from Joralemon would now remind the city gal that 'tis only among God's free hills that you can get an appetite, and then the author would say, 'Nothing had ever tasted so good as those trout, yanked from the brook and cooked to a turn on the sizzling coals.' " She looked at the stalwart young man, so skillfully frying the flapjacks, and contrasted him with the effeminate fops she had met on Fifth Avenue.[9]

This alternate milking and mocking of the conventions of the wilderness novel is a practice that Lewis carries on throughout *Free Air* as well as in the later *Mantrap* (1926). In *Free Air* Lewis includes realistic treatments of the primitive roads, temperamental automobiles, and the occasional filthy hotel and backroad degenerate. He also debunks Milt Daggett's pulp-fiction stereotype of aggressive lumberjacks wooing and winning reticent maidens. Nevertheless, the larger conception of nature and the West that emerges from the novel is not Claire Boltwood's early impression of "rocks and stumps and socks on the line," but rather is that familiar mythic territory for which Milt serves as emblem.[10]

Indeed, it is not nature as escape, but rather as birthright, that interests Lewis more. Nature serves most meaningfully in his novels as a means of connection to, and a reminder of the potentialities of, a pioneering heritage. Nature—more particularly the American upper Midwest—was the landscape on which a heroic new America was to be raised by creative and aspiring individuals, an important consideration to keep in mind while reading *Babbitt*. Such individuals emerge in Lewis's early romances like *The Trail of the Hawk* and *Free Air*. In both novels the protagonists' claim to a place in the new industrial society is based on their being creative technologists, students of the same scientific and engineering skills that had made folk heroes of Thomas Edison and Henry Ford. These are the gifts that were to transform the first transatlantic flight of Charles Lindbergh in 1927 into a technological epic. Interestingly, Lewis's hero, Carl Ericson of *The Trail of the Hawk*, is a pioneering aviator from Minnesota, and of Scandinavian stock, a remarkable anticipation of Lindbergh, who was born near Lewis's home town. In these early works, Lewis initiates a pattern of combining in his main characters natural and agrarian origins and values, together with the ability to mechanize successfully. Thus, Lewis absorbed perhaps the quintessential preindustrial emblem of American individualism, the self-sufficient Jeffersonian yeoman, into the industrial present of America.

Nature by itself was no longer relevant to the new urban-technological present and future. The midwesterner bound to the soil was an anachronism. If the American destiny of extending the western horizon was to be advanced, as Lewis believed, it would be by the native midwesterner who had grasped the new tools of science. Thus, Lewis joins writers like Hamlin Garland, Frank Norris, and Willa Cather in his belief that the old stalemate between machine and garden might be transformed into a progressive synthesis. And in this sense, Lewis is not merely lavishing exquisite praise on nature, as T. K. Whipple accused him of doing (Whipple 1928, 227). Rather, Lewis reaches toward the awareness of his culture-hero Henry David Thoreau that nature exists most meaningfully in relationship to the civilization of his time, rather than apart from it. Lewis was to give the yeoman-modern his most memorable depiction in the novel *Arrowsmith*. Martin Arrowsmith is everything that George F. Babbitt is not. Although Arrowsmith has sprung from the same rural Midwestern soil as Babbitt, the former becomes in turn a doctor, pathologist, and research scientist, and carries on the tradition of his pioneering forebears into a future in which he has renounced the comfortable success of a Babbitt for a cabin-laboratory in the Vermont woods. Intimations of scientific progress in *Arrowsmith* are both humanized and heightened in characteristic Lewis fashion by their associations with Jeffersonian individualism and nature.

In *Arrowsmith*, Lewis employed, for the only time, the solitary scientist as his hero. Characteristically, Lewis was to seek out less Olympian figures than the research scientist Arrowsmith for his studies of American life in the technological present. His main characters are likely to be those who suggest a pragmatic union of values, as revealed in their attempts to express their individualism within the social compact, as builders and makers. Correspondingly, Lewis would set his novels most often in his upper Midwest, in some version of his native Minnesota, which he described in an article in *The Nation* as "neither Western and violent, nor Eastern and crystallized," but which possessed, conversely, the virtues of western vigor with some claim to eastern finish.[11] The strain of idealism that defines Lewis's westerners seems a birthright of the region, of a land changed almost overnight from wilderness to advanced urban society:

> Seventy-five years ago—a Chippewa-haunted wilderness. Today— a complex civilization with a future which, stirring or dismayed or both, is altogether unknowable. To understand America it is merely necessary to understand Minnesota. But to understand Minnesota you must be an historian, an ethnologist, a poet, a cynic, and a graduate prophet all in one (*Man*, 285).

This central conception of mid-America as process rather than product, possessed of blind energy and latent potentiality, is repeatedly thrust before the reader of Lewis's novels. We see it in the opening of *Main Street*, where the young heroine stands on a hill where Indians camped two generations earlier, and she looks out over the mills and skyscrapers of Minneapolis and St. Paul, "the newest empire of the world," wondering at its future.[12] The same sense of undirected energy and possibility is repeated in the description of Babbitt's Floral Heights suburb, labored out of the wilderness a scant twenty years before Babbitt's time. We find it in Cass Timberlane's assertion that his city of Grand Republic "may be a new land for a new kind of people."[13]

We see it again in the hopefully named city of Newlife, where Lewis's final novel, *World So Wide*, opens. This protean power and potentiality is asserted strongly in Lewis's Nobel acceptance speech, where he described an America of enormous mountains, prairies, cities, and wealth, and yet possessed of a bewildering social complexity (*Man*, 17). Later he would call the rapid rise of a new civilization in the American Midwest the greatest possible challenge to a novelist (*Man*, 37).

Against his energized western landscapes and cityscapes, Lewis projects a great range of fictional figures, the most interesting of whom attempt to shape and direct their own lives in rhythm to the new culture emerging from their time of restless growth and change. Such a figure is Carol Kennicott, of *Main Street*. Because this novel immediately precedes *Babbitt*, and because the two novels are in many ways interrelated, it is useful to look briefly at the idealistic themes in *Main Street* before coming to terms with those in *Babbitt*.

Some readers, like H. L. Mencken, have seen Carol as only a flighty romantic, but the very quality of visionary dreaming that made her ridiculous to Mencken made her an appropriate heroine for Lewis, who clearly takes her seriously in the novel. What had begun for Carol during college as a sociology reading assignment—a text on town improvement—becomes a shadowy and ill-formed resolution to " 'get my hands on one of these prairie towns and make it beautiful' " (*Main Street*, 11). When she marries a small-town doctor, Will Kennicott, and moves with him to Gopher Prairie she seems to have the opportunity to carry out her dream. But she soon finds that what Will and the villagers have in mind by town improvement is cosmetic rather than surgical. Her ideas for raising the cultural level of the town extend beyond ideas for rebuilding. Will complains good-naturedly that she is " 'always spieling about how scientists ought to rule the world' " (381), an idea straight out of Thorstein Veblen, and she espouses other Progressive ideas. But she is presented to the reader primarily as a thwarted builder.

In the well-known passage in which she walks down Main Street for the first time, she notes, with the eye of the builder and planner, the ugliness, the "planlessness," the "temporariness," of the town, where "each man had built with the most valiant disregard of all the others" (41). Later, when she analyzes more carefully the town's shortcomings, it is with the eye of the visionary architect:

> She asserted that it is a matter of universal similarity; of flimsiness of construction, so that the towns resemble frontier camps; of neglect of natural advantages, so that the hills are covered with brush, the lakes shut off by railroads, and the creeks lined with dumping grounds; of depressing sobriety of color; rectangularity of buildings; and excessive breadth and straightness of the gashed streets, so that there is no escape from gales and from sight of the grim sweep of land, nor any windings to coax the loiterer along, while the breadth which would be majestic in an avenue of palaces makes the low shabby shops creeping down the typical Main Street the more mean by comparison (260).

Carol is a compelling figure for Lewis—and one who looks ahead to *Babbitt*—because of the extraordinary tension between the expectancy of her dreams and the forces of dullness and smugness that surround her. Shut off from any meaningful work by her position as woman and wife, her shallow education, her sentimentalism and flightiness, and her own sense of inadequacy to her task, she can bring her dreams to no real end. Schoolteacher Vida Sherwin's judgment against Carol that she is " 'an impossibilist. And you give up too easily' " (263), seems to have been shared by Lewis, to some extent. In a "sequel" to the novel that Lewis published in the *Nation* in 1924, Lewis surveys Gopher Prairie four years after the book ends and finds that a new school building "with its clear windows, perfect ventilation, and warm-hued tapestry brick," stands as testimony to Vida's low-pressure but persistent efforts to enact meaningful change (*Man*, 320). The Carol of the sequel, dumpy and defeated, has no such memorial to mark her fitful efforts at town improvement. And so Carol is resigned to her failure at the end of the novel: "She looked across the silent fields to the west. She was conscious of an unbroken sweep of land to the Rockies, to Alaska; a dominion which will rise to unexampled greatness when other empires have grown senile. Before that time, she knew, a hundred generations of Carols will aspire and go down in tragedy devoid of palls and solemn chanting, the humdrum inevitable tragedy of struggle against inertia" (*Main Street*, 431).

And so, at the end, no longer even the potential creator, Carol remains a frustrated figure living under a self-imposed truce with the town that she might have transformed into something distinctive and beautiful, had she possessed the technical skill and the nerve to match her idealism. Technical skill and nerve are, of course, the attributes of her doctor husband, Will, but without vision he remains merely the severed half of her incomplete self. What is called for in the wider design of *Main Street* is a sublime architect, a figure whose pragmatic technological mastery and courage to innovate are matched by the force of a dream. In *Babbitt*, Lewis was to mix these elements again in the unlikely figure of a middle-aged realtor who can find no adequate expression for his buried but insistent aspirations.

If *Main Street* shows us the potential builder deprived of the realization of her goal—a new town on the clean Midwestern horizon—*Babbitt* reverses the presentation to reveal the shining city actually achieved, but without an appropriate creator to shape or interpret its destiny. Both novels are concerned with defining a civilized existence for the citizens of a community. Both ask at what point in the process of civilization this humane life can be achieved. *Babbitt*'s Zenith has clearly gone beyond that point, as Carol Kennicott's Gopher Prairie has failed to reach it. Instead of *Main Street's* heroic natural landscape blighted by human incompetence and pettiness, *Babbitt* presents a human-created world of immense technological dazzle, but one devoid of meaningful human relationships, not only among its inhabitants, but between them and the products of their technology. It is a kind of upside-down *Walden*, where the buildings, houses, porcelain and tile bathrooms, and electric cigar lighters overwhelm the human figures and reduce their actions to insignificance. As he did in *Main Street*, Lewis was dramatizing in *Babbitt* the truth of Lewis Mumford's contemporary observation that "architecture and civilization develop hand in hand: the characteristic buildings of each period are the memorials to their dearest institutions."[14]

The magnificent Zenith skyline with which Lewis opens *Babbitt* suggests, as Lewis tells us, a city built for giants. But from this panoramic conception, the camera eye moves down, in a characteristically ironic Lewis coupling, to focus on the pathetic and helpless figure of George F. Babbitt, asleep in his Dutch Colonial house in the suburb of Floral Heights. From there the eye scans Babbitt's alarm clock, the gadgets in his bathroom, "so glittering and so ingenious that they resembled an electrical instrument-board," the eyeglasses, the suit, the contents of Babbitt's pockets—all of the wares by which the new city asserts its mastery over its inhabitants (8). While in *Main Street* we are shown the dream of a new civilization without the reality, in *Babbitt* we have the reality without the dream, a humming dynamo of a modern city whose external intimations of heroic accomplishment mock the meager-hearted citizens who inhabit it.

Lewis establishes a city that seems to offer great freedom and myriad opportunities for human achievement. At several points in *Babbitt* Lewis stops the narrative flow to give us a horizontal scan of the entire city of Zenith, bringing in, as we have seen, a montage of simultaneous events, vignettes of character and scene, ranging from low life to high, from urban despair to joy, from mindlessness to intellectual sophistication. The cumulative effect of these parallel scenes is to reveal the narrator's forthright and unslavish admiration for Zenith's potentialities. They seem to anticipate Lewis's own voicing of great expectations in the conclusion of his Nobel acceptance speech in 1930. There, he spoke of his joy in joining other American writers in a "determination to give to the America that has mountains and endless prairies, enormous cities and lost farm cabins, billions of money and tons of faith, to an America that is as strange as Russia and as complex as China, a literature worthy of her vastness" (*Man*, 17). Lewis's satiric realism in *Babbitt*, then, is placed against an urban landscape of great hope, a metropolis of boundless possibilities for human accomplishment.

It is important to recognize that George F. Babbitt instinctively responds to these visionary intimations. He palpitates in response to its complex systems. In his speeches to the Booster's Club, he loftily portrays the "realtor"—a newly coined term intended to clothe the low cunning of salesmanship with the mantle of the doc*tor*—as a far-sighted visionary, functioning as " 'a seer of the future development of the community, and as a prophetic engineer clearing the pathway for inevitable changes.' " Of course Babbitt is unable to translate this vision beyond its grossest commercial meaning, as Lewis underscores it for us, "that a real-estate broker could make money by guessing which way the town would grow" (38). Lewis puts Babbitt's ill-defined reverence for his metropolis into perspective by detailing his ignorance of Zenith's civic life, its social needs, its architecture, and his inability to *do* anything of a constructive or purposeful nature on its behalf. Babbitt is, as Lewis says, nimble only in the petty business of selling houses to people for more than they can afford to pay. Thus, Babbitt, with his monumental incompetence, is a perversion of Lewis's progressive dream. In a city built for giants, Babbitt, its representative man, is a midget. He can only barter structures; he cannot create them.

The distinction is important. Lewis clearly expects something more from his main figure. For George F. Babbitt is more than just the typical American businessman. He is also a westerner, and the western birthright, as Lewis's earlier works have demonstrated, is a significant one. As Lewis explained it elsewhere, the westerners may look like easterners; "both groups are chiefly reverent toward banking, sound Republicanism, the playing of golf and bridge, and the possession of large motors. But whereas the Easterner is content with these symbols and smugly desires nothing else, the Westerner, however golfocentric he may be, is not altogether satisfied. . . . secretly, wistfully he desires a beauty that he does not understand" (*Man*, 283).

Thus, we have Babbitt's vague but insistent yearning: " 'Wish I'd been a pioneer, same as my grand-dad,' " he muses at one point (75). At another, the outcast liberal attorney Seneca Doane touches Babbitt's secret, better self when he recalls their college days, when Babbitt was " 'an unusually liberal, sensitive chap. . . . you were going to be a lawyer, and take the cases of the poor for nothing, and fight the rich. And I remember I said I was going to be one of the rich myself, and buy paintings and live at Newport. I'm sure you inspired us all' " (244). Both Babbitt and Seneca Doane had graduated from college in the class of 1896, in the heady, early days of Progressive reform. But while Doane had gone on to live out Babbitt's dream, Babbitt had succumbed to the young Doane's meretricious visions of wealth. In this reversal of roles is to be found Babbitt's private admiration for Doane, and the basis for the realtor's transformation into a temporarily independent thinker in the latter part of the novel.

The reader notes that Babbitt is not alone in his western longings for a lost ideal. The theme of having failed one's own dreams of personal fulfillment, of having falsified one's noble goals, rings through the characterization of many of Babbitt's associates and acquaintances. Paul Riesling, Babbitt's best friend, has forsaken his love for the violin in order to spend his life selling tarpaper roofing. His sense of having betrayed his own self-worth is the bond that holds Babbitt to him. Chum Frink, the Eddie Guest doggerel poet, admits boozily that he has perverted his assumed talents, that he might have become a real poet (220). Ed Overbrook, the dismal insurance salesman, turns out to be another poet who has slipped off Parnassus (164). A salesman from Sparta whom Babbitt meets at the realtors' convention, "a grave, intense youngster," tells of his early dream of becoming a scientist (141).

We can add to these admitted closet idealists those whose failure to acknowledge the perversion of their own talents earns them Lewis's scorn. Babbitt's neighbor, Howard Littlefield, is one of these. With a Ph.D. in economics, he has reduced his scholarly and professional gifts to sanctifying the sordid money-grubbing tactics of Babbitt and his friends. " 'The guy who put the con in economics,' " chirps Babbitt brightly of Littlefield, whose field is little indeed (98). Then there are the ranks of bored and useless wives in the novel, women like Lucile McKelvey, Louetta Swanson, and Zilla Riesling, with nothing to do but vent their understandable dissatisfaction in flirtation or nagging. With no opportunity for a real life, their inner resources become so flaccid that they may fall victim, as does Zilla, to a barking religious hysteria.

Finally, in the novel's continuing interjection of marvelous counterfeits of contemporary magazine journalism and mail-order advertising—already noted for their satiric contributions—Lewis extends his gallery of dreamers to include an entire nation of upward-seekers, their tawdry pursuit of self-renewal unerringly mirrored in their mass media: manicure girls turned into movie stars, bootblacks become celebrated authors overnight, pale weaklings transformed magically into muscular he-men. Instant new careers in public speaking, in banking. Improve Your Memory! No Special Education Required! Errant but insistent visions of the might-have-been and the might-be are thus constantly projected into the larger social consciousness that Lewis portrays in *Babbitt*. The reader is presented with an America that is a version of what sociologist David Riesman was later to call "the lonely crowd," a veritable army of underachievers, all apparently marching to the same drummer, while they are unable to deny the seductive private rhythms of their own dreams, beating within their own skulls.

If Babbitt is a typical western dreamer, he is also strongly drawn, like all of Lewis's main characters, to nature. When Babbitt fantasizes over the romantic "fairy child" of his dreams, he inevitably imagines these trysts in natural settings—groves, gardens, moors, the sea. Even more striking are those occasions when, seeking the balms of nature and the release of male companionship, Babbitt heads off to the Maine woods. Here, he repeats the classic and familiar gesture of nonurban renewal for the American male, besieged by society. Even in the Maine woods, however, Babbitt cannot shake off the city that claims him. His dress and behavior in the woods are absurdly out of place: "[Babbitt] came out. . . . in khaki shirt and vast and flapping khaki trousers. It was excessively new khaki; his rimless spectacles belonged to a city office; and his face was not tanned but a city pink. He made a discordant noise in the place. But with infinite satisfaction he slapped his legs and crowed, 'Say, this is getting back home, eh?' " (124).

Babbitt's romantic conception of his Maine guide, Joe Paradise, as an incorruptible Leatherstocking and an appropriate model for Babbitt's own renewal in nature is destroyed when Joe reveals himself as a backwoods Babbitt. He will walk or canoe—reluctantly—to the best fishing places if the big-city sports insist. But he really prefers a flat-bottomed boat with an Evinrude outboard motor. Worse yet, he looks forward to the day when he can move to town and open up a shoe store. Thus Babbitt—too addled by his years of city life to absorb the regenerative silences of the woods, bereft by the loss of his friend Paul Riesling, and deprived, by Joe Paradise's feet (and shoe store) of clay, of an appropriate model of conduct in nature—is drawn back to his city as one who "could never run away from Zenith and family and office, because in his own brain he bore the office and the family and every street and disquiet and illusion of Zenith" (242).

Babbitt's retreat into nature fails as do his escapes into Tanis Judique's bohemianism and Seneca Doane's liberalism because his Zenith preoccupations have drained him of the values of hope and freedom that are his western birthright. He is thus incapable of grasping the terms of his dilemma. The call of the wild is indubitably real to Babbitt, as it has perhaps always been to Americans, but his fragmentary and childish conception of it (" 'moccasins—six-gun—frontier town—gamblers—sleep under the stars—be a regular man, with he-men like Joe Paradise—gosh!' ") renders him vulnerable to confusion and failure (238). The novel ends, as did *Main Street*, with a chastened rebel. But Babbitt remains at last a more pathetic figure than Carol Kennicott, for unlike her he is never able to formulate coherently the dream he is finally forced to deny.

7

Courting the Technological Sublime:
Babbitt's Dance

American writers from Thoreau onward have struggled with the contradictory meanings of a new machine civilization that they saw developing in America. Henry Adams, in his famous autobiography. *The Education of Henry Adams* (1918), had sardonically studied the purposeless power of the new age of machines and dynamos, and had contrasted what he saw as its insolent meaninglessness with the rich mystery of the medieval ages. Sinclair Lewis, too, was among those American novelists who attempted to read the meaning of a newly emerging technological America. In what follows, the pattern of romantic idealism in *Babbitt*—discussed in the preceding chapter—will be further explored as it relates to these issues of technology, power, and human control.

Babbitt engages us as an American novel because, among its other achievements, it depicts a central dilemma of modern times: the individual who is both in love with—and helpless before—the new technology that surrounds him. It is important in reading the novel to recognize the distinction Lewis constantly emphasizes between the high accomplishments of a technologically advanced civilization—as represented by the bold skyline of Zenith—and the soft-bellied underachievers who are the city's inhabitants. Where are the race of superior people that such a city seems to call for? Zenith, with its heartbeat of commerce, is a triumph of modern engineering and architecture, as Lewis makes clear in the novel's opening pages. The authorial voice, free of any irony, begins by praising the city's inspiring towers, "towers of steel and cement and limestone, sturdy as cliffs and delicate as silver rods" (5). Later in the opening chapter, Babbitt is raised to a pitch of almost religious exaltation while gazing out his window at the city spread out before him. "His slack chin lifted in reverence" for the shining limestone majesty of the Second National Tower. "Integrity was in the tower, and decision. It bore its strength lightly as a tall soldier" (14).

The adjectives and nouns applied to Zenith's commercial architecture here—"clean . . . austere . . . integrity . . . decision . . . strength"— suggest the qualities that identify Zenith itself as the heroic presence of the novel. Its great new buildings are admirable. They are unambiguous. They are ascendant. Rising above the sordid activities of its merchant class, the noble towers of Zenith announce the advent of a new kind of power in the world, and its transmutation into a fine and expressive new form. We respond as readers to this opening scene just as Babbitt and the narrator of the novel do, because it is part of our being human to wish to possess and command such power.

The same T. K. Whipple who wrote so perceptively as a critic of Lewis's work in 1928 also turned his attention to popular culture in America in a 1931 essay, "Machinery, Magic, and Art."[1] While Whipple does not discuss Lewis or his novels in this later essay, it has much relevance for readers of *Babbitt*. According to Whipple, the mechanical engineering of the early twentieth century prospered because it had clearly demonstrated the communication and control of power. In doing so, engineering and technology had assumed the crucial public function of art. And it did so largely because the arts themselves— particularly painting, music, and literature—had abandoned their public role in favor of individual expressions that were unintelligible to most of the public. In this climate, the pragmatic arts such as industrial design and architecture had thrived. These pragmatic arts taught us two lessons, said Whipple: "that any art can flourish if it will satisfy a strong universal desire; and that what [humans] crave is power" (Whipple 1943, 3). The origins of art, says Whipple, are the same as those of science and technology. Both go back to the same basic impulse that underlies the magic of primitive societies, the summoning up and exercising of actual or psychological power. In his provocative essay, Whipple compares the great achievements of modern science and engineering in making use of *natural* resources with the *potential* achievements of modern art in making use of *human* resources, had not contemporary art turned away from its traditional role of "conceiving powerful forms and images of more than personal significance" (Whipple 1943, 17).

This pairing of engineering and art, linking both with the identical human need to encompass and control power, suggests some new dimensions to Lewis's novel, and helps to account for the book's great popularity and appeal. Read from this perspective, *Babbitt* dramatizes remarkably the condition that Whipple describes: an ascendant technology within which the individual, deprived of the traditional function of a genuine art or mythology—to surcharge life with meaning—is left to feed on straw and chaff, and wonder why he is starving to death. If Babbitt's automobile is, as Lewis claims and demonstrates, his "poetry and tragedy," what profundities can he expect from it? Without any genuine artists, must Chum Frink, the doggerel poet of the newspapers, be left to serve as Zenith's only interpreter? In a city, Lewis tell us, built for giants, what creative void has left us with only a race of midgets? In the vast gulf in the America of 1922 between Zane Grey, on the one hand, and the obscure footnotes to "The Waste Land," on the other, where is the compelling communal artist who will shape the boundless energy of the new urban-industrial metropolis into a meaningful art for its inhabitants?

Babbitt, then, may be read as a study in personal impotence set against a cityscape full of the evidence of heroic technological power and achievement. One aspect of the curious appeal of George F. Babbitt as a character—and he seems always to have appealed to even those readers who found nothing tangible to admire in him—is his Gatsby-like capacity for wonder, the simple "passionate wonder" with which, as Lewis says, "he loved his city" (178). A major rhythmic pattern of the novel, established immediately in the opening pages, is Babbitt's mute reverence for Zenith. Babbitt loves the energy and creativity of his city, just as he is privately ashamed of the flaccid disorder and meaninglessness of his own personal life. As the book begins, Babbitt is, at one moment, rendered speechless by the nobility of Zenith's skyline. A few minutes later, he is reduced to frustration and comic incoherence by his bickering family at the breakfast table.

The high moments of Babbitt's day are those in which he is caught up and assigned a role—however minor—in the industrial drama of the city. Driving to work, he exults for the moment as his car is "banked with four others in a line of steel restless as cavalry, while the cross-town traffic, limousines and enormous moving-vans, and insistent motor-cycles, poured by. . . . He noted how quickly his car picked up. He felt superior and powerful, like a shuttle of polished steel darting in a vast machine" (45). Once he reaches his real-estate office, his malaise returns as he forces his attention to the ignoble art of pushing real estate. His spiritual ardor mounts again in an afternoon discussion with a customer about Babbitt's new cigar lighter: "He had enormous and poetic admiration, though very little understanding, of all mechanical devices. They were his symbols of truth and beauty. Regarding each new intricate mechanism—metal lathe, two-jet carburetor, machine gun, oxyacetylene welder—he learned one good realistic-sounding phrase, and used it over and over, with a delightful feeling of being technical and initiated" (58).

Standing in his bathroom, with its "sensational exhibit" of modern gadgetry, or buying gasoline at his service station and basking in the window display's agreeable glow of counterfeit wealth, "spark-plugs with immaculate porcelain jackets, tire-chains of gold and silver," Babbitt clearly demonstrates the persistent human impulse toward meaningful ardor, toward art, which he cannot find in his church, his family, his work, or his friends (8, 26). Ironically, as George F. Babbitt has been freed by technology from the toil of his pioneer grandfather, he has also been denied the experience of full participation in community life that made his forebears competent and integrated adults. As a result, he remains spiritually childish, as the frequent references to him as a baby make clear.

Babbitt's yearning and admiration for technology cannot be dismissed as the mere preoccupation of an addle-headed buffoon. For it is also a quality of the character in the novel who seems to be held in Lewis's highest regard. That character is Seneca Doane, the spokesman for the author's liberal heresies, who at one point argues with his houseguest, a European intellectual who decries the standardization of Zenith. Doane asserts stubbornly to his guest that " 'Zenith's a city with gigantic power—gigantic buildings, gigantic machines, gigantic transportation.' " And while Doane concedes that Zenith's standardization of minds must be fought against, he still admits, " 'sneakingly I have a notion that Zenith is a better place to live in than Manchester or Glasgow or Lyon or Berlin or Turin,' " and he insists that " 'I prefer a city with a future so unknown that it excites my imagination' " (84–85). The scene between Doane and his guest is part of a crosscutting series of simultaneous events that Lewis pans over with his camera-eye to demonstrate that Zenith is possessed of a diversity and excitement worthy of the serious artist's attention. Similarly, Lewis later in the novel writes of "the dozen contradictory Zeniths that together make up the true and complete Zenith" (174). The author suggests repeatedly the protean appeal of Zenith, subject to no single control, as its individual segments may be. There is a crucial distinction to be made here between the whole city of Zenith and the Zenith that is merely the sum of its parts. Lewis's satire is often directed against specific targets (Babbitt's drearily standardized house, for example, or the aggressively ostentatious Zenith Athletic Club), but the city itself is a more varied and richly textured creation, and it partakes of a deeper and more expressive meaning.

Babbitt's speech to the Zenith Real Estate Board is, for all of its ignorance and foolishness, a hymn of admiration and praise no less heartfelt than Huckleberry Finn's tribute to the Mississippi River, which sustains him and he loves. But Babbitt, drained of the personal qualities that might have allowed him to participate in and interpret more fully his urban world, is repeatedly driven to frustration and pettiness in his private and business life, or to escape into dreams of potency with his fairy child, or into unsatisfactory code-hero counterfeits of personal power as he heads off to the Maine woods where he wears his absurdly new khaki clothing for a week and boasts of the advantages of getting back to nature.

Set against a skyline of unmatchable achievement and potentiality, Babbitt's actions throughout the novel suggest a kind of exercise in failed religion. It is an unconsummated ritual whereby the power of the modern industrial order is courted by the main character, and this ritual is expressed through the imagery and rhythm of his interactions with the city and with the physical objects of modern urban existence. Like some primitive tribesman, as Whipple puts it, Babbitt seeks to internalize—to swallow—the power of the industrial deity that he sees all around him. He wants to release it within himself. He wants to express—to dance—his adoration for it. But his efforts to convert the surrounding world of objective physical energy into his own psychological and subjective potency fail because he cannot dance his attitude successfully. And there is no one, not priest or poet or sage, to show him how.

As Whipple claims, "Magic is the savage's engineering, his technology. It is his effort to get command of power and direct it to his own purposes" (Whipple 1943, 4). In this context, Babbitt's "magic" is ignorant and inept. Above all it is formless, and hence unsuccessful. For form is the means of making power useful. This is the sardonic lesson of all those evidences of industrial engineering, all those sublime buildings and wondrous machines and technological creations that draw Babbitt's rapt admiration. Inspired by the rhythm of his city, as we are told at the end of the novel's first chapter, "he beheld the tower as a temple-spire of the religion of business, a faith passionate, exalted, surpassing common men; and as he clumped down to breakfast he whistled the ballad 'oh, by gee, by gosh, by jingo,' as though it were a hymn melancholy and noble" (14–15). But of course it is not, and Babbitt's clumsy footwork here, and his nonsensical ditty are the evidence of his hieratical ineptitude. Lewis underscores the point through his own sure control of form in this passage, opening it with images of an earlier age of true faith and meaningful belief, suggested in the words "beheld" and "temple-spire," and in the Miltonic inversions of "a faith passionate, exalted, surpassing common men." Then Lewis reduces it all to comic absurdity, with Babbitt "clumping" down to the breakfast table to feed his insistently corporeal self while whis-tling—even the words are too much for him—a popular song of glos-salalial meaninglessness.

Lewis gives it all a last dig by repeating the adjective-noun inver-sions ("as though it were a hymn melancholy and noble") as a final ironic echo of this same structure earlier in the sentence. Babbitt's failed magic here, his incoherent attempts at expression, represent on the most ingenuous level what Lewis's text successfully demonstrates on the level of accomplished artistry—the embodying of rhythm and image in an incantation for capturing the power latent in the situation. Lewis as artist-novelist underlines Babbitt's dilemma by depicting his main character's futile attempts to shape his life—or his response to his life—into some sort of coherent form, against the background of a well-made object, the novel *Babbitt* itself. The novel messages its own medium as it proceeds, reminding us that as technology solves the problems of the physical world through intelligent and efficient design and engineering, art becomes increasingly necessary in channel-ing the power inherent in these developments into communicable and meaningful form.

The shadow of Thorstein Veblen once again falls across the novel not only in the book's classic depiction of "conspicuous consumption" but also in Babbitt's yearnings for the lost sense of a healthy relation-ship to his work, a trait that Veblen had called "the instinct of work-manship." For Veblen, this instinct was a primary motivation for human behavior and the basis for a just and moral society.[2] Babbitt reveals vestigial shreds of this instinct, swelling with pride and loving with passion the creations of his world. Yet, as Veblen had illustrated in an earlier work, Babbitt was prevented from recovering the lost instinct of workmanship by the intervention of an acquisitive business system that worked inexorably to separate the marketing and control of goods from those who create them. The dilemma of Babbitt's alien-ation in this regard is further heightened by his occupation as salesman, which Veblen had called "the most conspicuous, and perhaps the gravest, of those wasteful and industrially futile practices that are involved in the businesslike conduct of industry."[3]

Thus, it might be said that Babbitt is the antihero of his heroic city, and that the real hero never appears. The shadow-hero of *Babbitt*, the figure who never appears yet whose presence is felt in the noble towers of Zenith's skyline, is the consummate architect-designer who conceived all of this and brought it into being. Inevitably, the result of having the triumphant designs of Zenith held before us is to draw our attention to their creator. "Form will communicate," says student of design Robert F. Pile, "irrespective of its maker's desire, because the human sensory system never stops searching out the meaning dis- coverable in any reality."[4] But in addition to the meaning-making tendencies of those who read the grandeur of the Zenith skyline, there is the further impetus toward meaning in the sense that an architecture that communicates so powerfully bespeaks a powerful motive to com- municate on the part of the maker. Why, then, is this shadow-hero of the new technology withheld in *Babbitt*?

The question looms larger when we return to the fact that the architect-designer-builder is a figure around which Lewis fashioned a number of his novels, from the beginning to the end of his career. He went on from the inventor and designer hero Carl Ericson of the early novel *The Trial of the Hawk*, to Milt Daggett, the mechanic and embryonic engineer of *Free Air*, to *Main Street*'s Carol Kennicott, the frustrated town-planner of a garden-city on the Minnesota prairies. After *Babbitt* and the scientist hero of *Arrowsmith* (1925), Lewis presented in *Dodsworth* (1929) the fullest treatment of the heroic builder. Sam Dodsworth, fifty-year-old automobile maker, decides in that novel to do something more with the rest of his life than build automobiles. He is ready as the novel progresses to devote himself to the designing and building of "noble houses that would last three hundred years, and not be scrapped in a year, as cars were."[5] Although *Dodsworth* is the culmination of Lewis's efforts to bring forth a vision- ary western creative technologist, the novel reveals a troublesome lessening of intensity toward its main theme, an inability or unwilling- ness to follow Sam Dodsworth the heroic builder through to the com- pletion of his grand designs. *Dodsworth* closes with the continuing promise of a new life for Sam, but he has now bounced from wooded estates to travel trailers, which he had earlier imagined as carrying urbanites in comfort into the forest. " 'Kind of a shame to have 'em ruin any more wilderness. (Oh, that's just sentimentality,' he assured himself.") (27). And houses or trailers, we are never witness to their creation. Nor do they quite qualify for their role, however much they might widen the vistas of nature-hungry Americans. The earlier dream of a Carol Kennicott, hazy as it was, embraced the entire community in a gesture of democratic inclusiveness, rather than just the comfortably well-off portion of it to which Sam Dodsworth has limited himself.

In such curiously diminished forms, creators and builders continue to appear in Lewis's later novels. Myron Weagle of *Work of Art* (1934), for example, rebuilds a hotel in a small Kansas town and turns it into the creation celebrated in the book's title. It is to be seen as a "work of art," as opposed to the cheap and meretricious books turned out by his writer brother. But after the larger design of Lewis's earlier works, a hotel keeper, however proficient, scarcely qualifies as significant builder, nor does his western inn begin to fill the expansive canvas that Lewis has prepared. In *The God-Seeker* (1949), Lewis exchanges new pioneering for old, but the pattern of reduction remains. Aaron Gadd abandons the larger dream that has sent him west to the Minnesota frontier in the nineteenth century and he returns to his trade of carpentry: " 'There are many things I don't ever expect to know, and I'm not going to devote myself to preaching about them but to building woodsheds so true and tight that they don't need ivory and fine gold— straight white pine, cedar shingles, a door that won't bind—glorious!' "[6]

Finally, in his last novel, *World So Wide* (1951), Lewis introduces an architect-hero whose dream is to build a skyscraper village, "the first solution in history of rural isolation and loneliness."[7] Yet the dream is rather oddly abandoned early in the novel. Lewis had first advanced the idea of the office building as a new kind of village and community in the third chapter of *Babbitt*. And the plans for an actual skyscraper community were to be found on the desk of Frank Lloyd Wright, in a striking parallel between the thinking of Lewis and the visionary midwestern architect. Wright's towering skyscraper, "The Mile-High Illinois," a cantilevered shaft of 528 stories was to have been a "sky-city," another attempt, like Lewis's, to redefine human relationships through the projection of bold new architectural structures on the clean Midwestern landscape.[8] Both designs still await their builder.

Thus, Lewis seems to have been compelled toward the builder-hero, but nowhere does that figure emerge in full form. Nowhere does Lewis actually give us a central figure whose idealism is matched by a demonstrable and functioning mastery of the urban-industrial order. Lewis's novels give us many unrealized or fragmentary versions of this figure, but with the possible exception of Martin Arrowsmith, whose scientific achievements are less tangible than those of the architect-builder, the grand designer never fulfills the expectations suggested at the start.

But of course Lewis's artistic achievements attain their own conse-quentiality, apart from that of his fictional heroes and heroines. One measure of the artistic superiority of *Babbitt* in the Lewis canon may be in the author's resistance to what was for him almost an obligatory creative hero, but one whom Lewis could never make fully convincing. *Babbitt*'s success as a novel is attributable in part to this gap in Lewis's text: the withholding of the characteristic builder-hero, the figure who compelled Lewis's allegiance at the same time that it defied full and credible depiction in his works. Lewis's denial of this figure in *Babbitt* is not total, for the insistent creator does appear in the novel, if only briefly at the conclusion. He emerges in the form of Babbitt's son, Ted, Theodore Roosevelt Babbitt, whose name resonates with his father's not-quite-forgotten aspirations toward Progressive action and the manly western virtues. Ted, the rebellious would-be inventor and natu-ral-born mechanic, vows to follow his own talents and suggests a more hopeful future as the new technocrat rising from the ashes of Babbitt's life. Mercifully, though, Lewis spares us anything beyond a glimpse of Ted's future. As a teenage husband with a movie-fan wife, an entry-level factory job, and no education, his prospects do not bear close examination.

Thus, the brilliant inversion of Lewis's idealism that is *Babbitt* stands as a negative counterpoint to the great survey of American technological civilization in its rampant phase, which was Lewis's own heroic fabrication, as seen in the total body of his novels. As a commu-nal and vernacular artist, hence as a wielder of power in the older and traditional sense, Lewis affirms the possibility for individual control over the emerging industrial juggernaut, the sort of powerful role sought by so many of his fictional characters. Ironically, it is Lewis's antihero, Babbitt, who remains his indisputable contribution to the ages, and the leaderless, anonymous Zenith that joins and perhaps surpasses Main Street as his most memorable setting.

8

Lewis and Babbitt—Two American Lives

William Rose Benét tells of how he and Sinclair Lewis once met a traveling salesman, and of how Lewis entered into a long conversation with the man, while Benét remained disapprovingly aloof. " 'That's the trouble with you, Bill,' said Lewis afterwards, 'you regard him as hoi polloi, he doesn't even represent the cause of labor or anything dramatic—but I understand that man—by God, I love him.' "[1]

If it is true, as has often been said of Lewis, that he is more interesting as a mocking satirist than as an earnest idealist, it is also evident that without the counterforce of affirmation, Lewis's novels—and especially *Babbitt*—would not be the works that they are. Lewis was indeed, as he claimed, a "fanatic American," and his passion for America extended both to its achievements and its shortcomings. In Lewis we see shared strains of two characteristic American voices: the Jeremiad scourging of our national failings and the optimistic celebration of our potentialities.[2] The two currents in Lewis's thought may be roughly traced to his principal nineteenth-century forebears, Thoreau and Emerson.

Curiously, though, despite Lewis's oft-stated praise of Thoreau and his corresponding disparagement of Emerson, it is Emerson who emerges most strongly from Lewis's work, and Emerson who might have provided Lewis with a shock of recognition, had he read the Concord sage more carefully.[3] Lewis precisely echoes Emerson's belief that a civilization is to be judged by the extent to which it draws the most benefit from its cities. Like Emerson, Lewis sees nature and the city as ultimately reconcilable through the city's being related more closely to its natural environment. Like Emerson, he envisions this reconciliation as the role of a heroic figure—a Babbitt with brains—who will fulfill his own destiny and that of the nation in carrying out this synthesis. Like Emerson, Lewis conceived of this figure as a western cosmopolitan, one who would combine within himself natural and urban attributes. Finally, like Emerson, Lewis's emblem for the American future is what Michael Cowan, in his study of Emerson, calls a "City of the West," a combining and reconciling of industrial and Arcadian values.[4]

In his commitment to progress, Lewis comes into sharp conflict with Thoreau, who stood grimly on the side of nature in what he often depicted as a virtual state of warfare between the countryside and the city. Lewis, on the other hand, can hardly restrain his enthusiasm in the presence of advancing civilization:

> My delight in watching the small Middle Western cities grow, sometimes beautifully and sometimes hideously, and usually both together, from sod shanties to log huts to embarrassed-looking skinny white frame buildings, may be commented on casually. There is a miracle in the story of how all this has happened in two or three generations. Yet, after this period, which is scarcely a second in historic time, we have a settled civilization with traditions and virtues and foolishness as fixed as those of the oldest tribe of Europe. I merely submit that such a theme is a challenge to all the resources a novelist can summon. (*Man*, 37)

Here is Lewis's own version of Babbitt's speech to the Real Estate Board. In its Emersonian affirmation of hopeful possibilities is the key to Lewis's—and our—reservoir of good feeling toward Babbitt. For all of his flaws, Lewis cannot quite disdain Babbitt's unflagging belief in the potentialities of American life. No less fanatic an American than his creator, Babbitt is bred in the bone of Lewis's own commitment to a progressive American tomorrow. As Emerson himself put it, in yet another version of the same architectural and urban imperative that Lewis and Babbitt express three generations later,

> The history of any settlement is an illustration of the whole—first the emigrant's camp, then the group of log cabins, then the cluster of white wooden towns . . . and almost as soon followed by brick and granite cities, which in another country would stand for centuries, but which here must soon give way to enduring marble. (Cited in Cowan, 26)

There is a visionary in all three men, though with Babbitt, of course, the hopeful seer can never quite shed the dollar-sign scales from his eyes.

Lewis's tendency to identify himself publicly with his more admirable fictional creations (e.g., Carl Ericson, Carol Kennicott, Martin Arrowsmith) suggests rather pointedly that we may also find in Babbitt a surrogate for his creator's romantic and idealistic qualities, as well as the embodiment of those hateful tendencies that forever divert the pilgrim from his goal. Whether Lewis portrays the worthwhile life in America explicitly—in the hopes and dreams of a character like Babbitt, or implicitly—in the aspects of Babbitt's life that Lewis selects for attack, the idealist and satirist in him merge in the moral basis from which both the idealism and the satire proceed.

Somewhere, Lewis believed, in the progression of American life from the sod shanty to the asphalt parking lot, we had missed civilization. But perhaps it was still not too late. Like the older political Progressives at the turn of the century, with whom Lewis spiritually belongs, he saw the historical process as capable of transcending the tragic decline of American potentialities into the shallow selfishness of the urban-industrial juggernaut. Through the body of his novels, and perhaps most memorably in *Babbitt*, Lewis asserts the prodigious energy with which the country was growing and changing. He reveals his belief that the culture that emerged from this ferment might yet be shaped and heightened by such fictional figures as he created, as Babbitt wished to be, and by such a writer as he himself wished to be. Thus, we have his revealing confession to Perry Miller that " 'I love America. . . . I love it, but I don't like it,' " and his repeated claim that he wanted to raise the cultural maturity of America by mocking its "cruder manifestations."[5] When he ridiculed and satirized American mythologies, he did so only when they had become empty apologies for present mediocrity, rather than the spirit by which our national possibilities might be advanced.

Sinclair Lewis attempted a great survey of American life as it passed swiftly into its modern phase. In *Main Street, Arrowsmith, Dodsworth*—and in *Babbitt*, where satiric inversions jostle with hopeful dreams—Lewis demonstrated his rightful claim to a place among those writers who have examined the sources of validity in American life, and who have created in their works new emblems of possibility to be measured against the failures of the present.

Looking back at the preceding chapters, and considering all of the often-conflicting aspects that *Babbitt* contains, the reader might well conclude that the novel is a generic puzzle. Is it a realistic work? a sociological slice of life? a comedy built around a figure of Falstaffian vigor and resilience? a satire, both toothless and biting? a romance? a tragedy? an urban myth in which the heroic city seeks its own creator? *Babbitt* has the pictorial accuracy of a mirror image, but is such reproduction art? Its sound track is a triumph of mimicry, but can mimicry amount to more than a brief diversion? *Babbitt* presents itself as social realism, but on closer examination it is seen to violate the principal tenet of realism, that the author be backgrounded and, insofar as is possible, seem to disappear. The fabric of social reality is certainly essential in a work in which the main character is determined by the social code, but the author is so clearly and creatively on the attack against the values of the system that we must consider the work as a satire. But satire requires a militant moral tone and a willingness to deal only with surfaces, lest by looking beneath the surface of the satiric target, the reader's scorn is softened by an infusion of sympathy. Yet Lewis the satirist *does* dive down beneath Babbitt's exterior conformity and complacency to reveal a romantic yearner who desires more than he understands. And in that yearning, we perceive a kind of vestigial worth, a solidity and decency in Babbitt's basic nature that silences our derisive laughter. No man is a hypocrite in his pleasures, said Samuel Johnson, and in Babbitt's mute yearnings for nature, or in his inarticulate delight and ignorant dedication to the technological power that surrounds him, we find a shadow of the purposeful creator he might have been. There is a tragic element in this, but unlike the tragic figure, Babbitt lives, and, in the characteristic fashion of the realist hero, muddles through.

By the logic of the genres, *Babbitt* is a failure. But art is cleverer than criticism, and the generic categories must always be set against the unique, and unclassifiable qualities of the individual work of art. A fictional work that corresponds exactly to a single formal category may still be quite dead for its readers, while *Babbitt* has remained a lively and engrossing experience—a good read—for several generations of audiences, and its title figure still holds on to his place within the lexicon of English speakers. The delusions of enjoyment have their own authenticity, and they reflect, like Lewis's resilient hero himself, the multitudinous means by which the bright and elusive book of life may be expressed.

Clearly, Lewis has not fulfilled the popular prediction of fifty years ago that, of all those American writers then living, he was the most likely to be considered a "classic" by the year 2000. Still, he has given us in each of his best novels, and above all in *Babbitt*, a work that is indispensable in American literature and culture. A book of many strands of aesthetic and social significance, *Babbitt* is also a work of love, a mocking and yet heroic authentication of the fanatic American-ness of its author. Mark Schorer concludes in his monumental biography of Lewis that "without his writing one cannot imagine modern American literature" (1961, 813). Applying this judicious evaluation to Lewis's masterwork, it is tempting to add that no one can claim to understand American life in the twentieth century without having read *Babbitt*.

Notes and References

Babbitt and the Twenties

1. Felix Frankfurter, "The Crime of Radicalism," in *The Culture of the Twenties*. ed. Loren Baritz (Indianapolis: Bobbs-Merrill). 122: hereafter cited in text.

2. Hiram Wesley Evans, "The KKK," in Baritz, 104.

3. Malcolm Cowley, *Exile's Return: A Literary Odyssey of the 1920's* (New York: Viking Press, 1951; Compass Books, 1956), 7.

4. Sinclair Lewis, "The American Fear of Literature" (Nobel Prize Address), in *The Man from Main Street: Selected Essays and Other Writings: 1904–1950*, ed. Harry E. Maule and Melville H. Cane (New York: Random House: Pocket Books, 1963), 17; hereafter cited in text as *Man*.

Capturing the Archetype

1. *The Random House Dictionary of the English Language: College Edition*, ed. Laurence Urdang (New York: Random House, 1968), 97.

2. Joseph Wood Krutch, "Sinclair Lewis," in *Sinclair Lewis: A Collection of Critical Essays*, ed. Mark Schorer (Englewood Cliffs, N.J.: Prentice-Hall, 1962), 147.

3. Quoted in Mark Schorer, *Sinclair Lewis: An American Life* (New York: McGraw-Hill, 1961), 349; hereafter cited in text.

4. Vernon Louis Parrington, *Main Currents in American Thought, vol. III: The Beginnings of Critical Realism in America: 1860–1920* (New York: Harcourt, Brace and World, 1930; Harbinger Books, 1958), 360–61.

5. Sinclair Lewis, *Babbitt* (New York: Harcourt, Brace, 1922; New American Library Signet Classic, 1962), 95; hereafter cited in text.

6. Sinclair Lewis, "Unpublished Introduction to *Babbitt*," in Lewis, *Man*, 22–23.

Babbitt and the Critics

1. Carl Van Doren, *Three Worlds* (New York: Harper and Brothers, 1936), 146.

2. Sinclair Lewis, *From Main Street to Stockholm: Letters of Sinclair Lewis. 1919–1930,* ed. Harrison Smith (New York: Harcourt, Brace, 1952), 59.

3. May Sinclair, "The Man from Main Street," *The New York Times Book Review and Magazine* (section 3, Sunday, 24 Sept. 1922), 10–11.

4. Upton Sinclair, "Standardized America," in *The Merrill Studies in Babbitt* (Columbus, Ohio: Charles E. Merrill, 1971), 29.

5. Stuart P. Sherman, in "It Seems Good Enough," *New York Times Book Review and Magazine* (section 3, Sunday, 24 Sept. 1922), 11.

6. H. L. Mencken, "Portrait of an American Citizen," in *Sinclair Lewis: A Collection of Critical Essays,* ed. Mark Schorer (Englewood Cliffs, N.J.: Prentice-Hall, 1962), 20; hereafter cited in text.

7. For a full consideration of the commercial films made from Lewis's work see Wheeler Dixon, "Cinematic Adaptations of the Works of Sinclair Lewis," in *Sinclair Lewis at 100: Papers Presented at a Centennial Conference,* ed. Michael E. Connaughton (St. Cloud, Minnesota: St. Cloud State University, 1985), 191–97.

8. T. K. Whipple, *Spokesmen* (New York: D. Appleton, 1928), 219; hereafter cited in text.

9. Constance Rourke, *American Humor* (New York: Harcourt, Brace, 1931; Doubleday Anchor Books, 1953), 223–24.

10. For a fuller account of Lewis and the Nobel Prize, see Sheldon Grebstein. "Sinclair Lewis and the Nobel Prize," *Western Humanities Review* 13 (Spring 1959): 163–71, and the discussion in Grebstein's *Sinclair Lewis* (New York: Twayne, 1962), 117–21.

11. Alfred Kazin, *On Native Grounds* (New York: Harcourt, Brace, 1942; Doubleday Anchor Books, 1956), 173; hereafter cited in text.

12. Jack L. Davis, "Mark Schorer's Sinclair Lewis," *Sinclair Lewis Newsletter* 3 (1971): 3–9. Schorer's 1969 essay on *Babbitt,* entitled "Sinclair Lewis's *Babbitt,*" originally appeared in *Landmarks of American Writing,* ed. Hennig Cohen (New York: Basic Books, 1969), 315–27. Schorer's 1969 essay is also reprinted in *The Merrill Studies in Babbitt,* ed. Martin Light (Columbus, Ohio: Charles E. Merrill, 1971).

13. M. Gilbert Porter, "From Babbitt to Rabbit: The American Materialist in Search of a Soul," in *American Literature in Belgium,* ed. Gilbert Debusscher (Amsterdam: Rodopi, 1987), 185–96.

Babbitt and Realism

1. Rene Wellek, *Concepts of Criticism* (New Haven: Yale University Press, 1963), 240–41.

2. Edward Abbey, *Desert Solitaire* (New York: Random House, 1968: Ballantine Books, 1988), 111–12.

3. Gerald Graff, "The Politics of Anti-Realism," *Salmagundi* 42 (Summer-Fall 1978): 4; hereafter cited in text.

4. Ralph Waldo Emerson, *Selected Prose and Poetry*, Second Edition, ed. Reginald L. Cook (San Francisco: Rinehart Press, 1968), 28.

5. J. P. Sterne, *On Realism* (London: Routledge and Kegan Paul, 1973), 108; hereafter cited in text.

6. Philip K. Dick, *I Hope I Shall Arrive Soon* (London: Victor Gollancz, Ltd., 1986), 4.

7. Tom Wolfe, "Stalking the Billion-Footed Beast," *Harper's* 279 (November 1989): 55; hereafter cited in text.

8. See Helen Batchelor, "A Sinclair Lewis Portfolio of Maps: Zenith to Winnemac," *Modern Language Quarterly* 32 (December 1971): 401–08.

9. Mark Schorer, "Sinclair Lewis: *Babbitt*," in *Landmarks of American Writing*, ed. Hennig Cohen (New York: Basic Books, 1969), 316–17.

Satire and Style in *Babbitt*

1. In *Humor in America: An Anthology*, ed. Enid Veron (New York: Harcourt Brace Jovanovich, 1976), 260.

2. Ambrose Bierce, *The Devil's Dictionary* (New York: Neale, 1911; Dover Books, 1962), 119.

3. Richard Bridgman, "Satire's Changing Target," *College Composition and Communication* 16 (May 1965): 85–89.

4. Herman Melville, *Typee; The Writings of Herman Melville: The Northwestern-Newberry Edition*, vol. I (Evanston and Chicago: Northwestern University Press and The Newberry Library, 1968), 169.

5. For a thorough treatment of the changing image of the small town in American literature, see Anthony Channell Hilfer, *The Revolt from the Village* (Chapel Hill: University of North Carolina Press, 1969).

6. Mark Twain, "The Mysterious Stranger," in *Great Short Works of Mark Twain*, ed. Justin Kaplan (New York: Harper and Row Perennial Classics, 1967), 360.

7. T. J. Matheson rightly corrects those critics who misread Lewis's satiric techniques as evidence of flawed realism. See Matheson's "Misused Language: The Narrator's Satiric Function in Sinclair Lewis's *Babbitt*," in *Sinclair*

Lewis at 100: Papers Presented at a Centennial Conference (St. Cloud, Minnesota; St. Cloud State University, 1985), 35–43; hereafter cited in text.

8. E. B. White, "Across the Street and into the Grill," in *The Second Tree from the Corner* (New York: Harper, 1953).

Impossible Dreams: *Babbitt* and Romance

1. Sanford E. Marovitz, "Ambivalences and Anxieties: Character Reversals in Sinclair Lewis's *Mantrap*," *Studies in American Fiction* 16 (Autumn 1988): 234.

2. Sherwood Anderson, "Four American Impressions," *The New Republic* 32 (October 11, 1922): 172.

3. Maurice Kramer, "Sinclair Lewis and the Hollow Center," in *The Twenties: Poetry and Prose*, ed. Richard E. Langford and William E. Taylor (Deland, Florida: Everett Edwards, 1966), 69.

4. The "contradiction . . ." statement is from Lewis's "Unpublished Introduction to *Babbitt*" (See *Man* 26). Lewis's self-description is from "The Death of Arrowsmith," *Coronet* 10 (July 1941): 108.

5. Sinclair Lewis, "The Greatest American Novelist," *Newsweek* 11 (January 3, 1938): 29.

6. For Lewis's praise of Thoreau and *Walden*, see "Introduction to *Four Days on the Webutuck River*," in *Man*, 169–70, and "One-Man Revolution," *Man*, 242–44.

7. The wilderness rehabilitation at its most strained is found in Lewis's later work, *The Prodigal Parents* (1938), where Fred Cornplow rescues his dull-witted son from sloth and dissipation by forcing him into a canoe trip through the Canadian wilderness. With greater restraint, however, Lewis (himself an inveterate walker) will portray, in *Main Street* and *Dodsworth*, the hike through the countryside as a convincing effort by his characters to break away from destructive and inhibiting social pressures.

8. *The Job* (New York: Harcourt, Brace, 1917), 203.

9. *The Trail of the Hawk* (New York: Harcourt, Brace, 1915), 316–17.

10. *Free Air* (New York: Harcourt, Brace, 1919), 190.

11. Sinclair Lewis, "Minnesota, the Norse State," *The Nation* 116 (May 30, 1923): 624; hereafter cited in text.

12. Sinclair Lewis, *Main Street* (New York: Harcourt, Brace, 1920), 28; hereafter cited in text.

13. Sinclair Lewis, *Cass Timberlane* (New York: Random House, 1945), 28.

14. Lewis Mumford, *Sticks and Stones* (New York: Boni and Liveright, 1924; Dover Books, 1955), 87.

Courting the Technological Sublime: Babbitt's Dance

1. T. K. Whipple, "Machinery, Magic, and Art," in his *Study Out the Land* (Berkeley: University of California Press, 1943), 1–18; hereafter cited in text.

2. Thorstein Veblen, *The Instinct of Workmanship* (New York: Macmillan, 1914).

3. Thorstein Veblen, *The Engineers and the Price System* (New York: Viking, 1921), 109.

4. Robert F. Pile, *Design: Purpose, Form, and Meaning* (Amherst: University of Massachusetts Press, 1979), 96.

5. Sinclair Lewis, *Dodsworth* (New York: Harcourt, Brace, 1929; New American Library Signet Edition, 1967), 182; hereafter cited in text.

6. Sinclair Lewis, *The God-Seeker* (New York: Popular Library, 1949), 307.

7. Sinclair Lewis, *World So Wide* (New York: Random House, 1951), 9.

8. Frank Lloyd Wright, *A Testament* (New York: Horizon Press, 1957), 238–48.

Lewis and Babbitt—Two American Lives

1. D. J. Dooley, *The Art of Sinclair Lewis* (Lincoln: University of Nebraska Press, 1967), 241.

2. The two strains have been most recently elucidated in Sacvan Berkovitch's *The American Jeremiad* (Madison: University of Wisconsin Press, 1978).

3. For Lewis's praise of Thoreau, see ch. 6, n. 6. For Lewis's disparagement of Emerson, see Lewis's Nobel acceptance speech (*Man*, 15) and "One-Man Revolution" (*Man*, 243).

4. I am indebted to Michael Cowan's *City of the West: Emerson, America, and the Urban Metaphor* (New Haven: Yale University Press, 1967), for my understanding of Emerson in this context; hereafter cited in text.

5. Perry Miller, "The Incorruptible Sinclair Lewis," *The Atlantic* 187 (April 1951): 34.

Selected Bibliography

Primary Sources

Hike and the Aeroplane. New York: Stokes, 1912. Published under the pseudonym Tom Graham.

Our Mr. Wrenn. New York: Harper, 1914.

The Trail of the Hawk. New York: Harper, 1915.

The Job. New York: Harper, 1917.

The Innocents. New York: Harper, 1917.

Free Air. New York: Harcourt, Brace, 1919.

Main Street. New York: Harcourt, Brace, 1920.

Babbitt. New York: Harcourt, Brace, 1922.

Arrowsmith. New York: Harcourt, Brace, 1925.

Mantrap. New York: Harcourt, Brace, 1926.

Elmer Gantry. New York: Harcourt, Brace, 1927.

The Man Who Knew Coolidge. New York: Harcourt, Brace, 1928.

Dodsworth. New York: Harcourt, Brace, 1929.

Ann Vickers. Garden City, N.Y.: Doubleday, Doran, 1933.

Work of Art. Garden City, N.Y.: Doubleday, Doran, 1934.

Selected Short Stories. Garden City, N.Y.: Doubleday, Doran, 1935.

Jayhawker. Garden City, N.Y.: Doubleday, Doran, 1935.

It Can't Happen Here. Garden City, N.Y.: Doubleday, Doran, 1935.

The Prodigal Parents. Garden City, N.Y.: Doubleday, Doran, 1938.

Bethel Merriday. Garden City, N.Y.: Doubleday, Doran, 1940.

Gideon Planish. New York: Random House, 1943.

Selected Bibliography

Cass Timberlane. New York: Random House, 1945.

Kingsblood Royal. New York: Random House, 1947.

The God-Seeker. New York: Random House, 1949.

World So Wide. New York: Random House, 1951.

From Main Street to Stockholm: Letters of Sinclair Lewis, 1919–1930. Selected and with an introduction by Harrison Smith. New York: Harcourt, Brace, 1952.

The Man from Main Street: A Sinclair Lewis Reader, Selected Essays and Other Writings, 1904–1950. Edited by Harry E. Maule and Melville H. Cane. New York: Random House, 1953.

I'm a Stranger Here Myself and Other Stories. New York: Dell, 1962.

Storm in the West. New York: Stein and Day, 1963.

Secondary Sources

Books

Bucco, Martin, ed. *Critical Essays on Sinclair Lewis.* Boston: G. K. Hall, 1986. The most recent collection of criticism on Sinclair Lewis. Includes a helpful and thorough introduction tracing the development of Lewis criticism from the earliest reviews to the present.

Connaughton, Michael E., ed. *Sinclair Lewis at 100: Papers Presented at a Centennial Conference.* St. Cloud, Minnesota: St. Cloud State University, 1985. Gathers papers given at the Lewis Centennial. Fresh, recent views on *Main Street, Babbitt,* and several other novels, as well as valuable essays on style, pedagogy, and films made from Lewis novels, etc.

Dooley, D. J. *The Art of Sinclair Lewis.* Lincoln: University of Nebraska Press, 1967. Examines Lewis's paradoxical mind and its reflection in the generic puzzles often demonstrated in his novels. Enthusiastically delineates Lewis's strengths and weaknesses, giving particular attention to *Babbitt.*

Grebstein, Sheldon Norman. *Sinclair Lewis.* New York: Twayne, 1962. A sound and thorough overview of Lewis's life and works. Coming at a time when Lewis's work was devalued, Grebstein properly emphasizes the writer's best work in the decade of the 1920s.

Lewis, Grace Hegger. *With Love from Gracie: Sinclair Lewis, 1912–1925.* New York: Harcourt, Brace, 1955. Excellent biographical portrait by Lewis's first wife. An important source of information about Lewis's days of early struggle and sudden fame.

Light, Martin, ed. *The Merrill Studies in Babbitt.* Columbus, Ohio: Charles

E. Merrill, 1971. Collects Lewis's comments on *Babbitt* and a range of critical essays on the novel, including two insightful pieces, not previously printed, on satire in the novel.

————. *The Quixotic Vision of Sinclair Lewis*. West Lafayette, Indiana: Purdue University Press, 1975. Sees the conflict between romance and realism in Lewis as an expression of quixotism, after the famous work, *Don Quixote*, by Cervantes. Thus, Lewis lacked a firm context for modern thought.

Lundquist, James. *The Merrill Guide to Sinclair Lewis*. Columbus, Ohio: Charles E. Merrill, 1970. Short guide to Lewis's novels and an overview of his contribution to American literature.

————. *Sinclair Lewis*. New York: Frederick Ungar, 1973. Helpful, short overview of Lewis's career, reacting, in part, to the "exaggerated melodrama" of Lewis's life, as depicted by Schorer and others.

O'Connor, Richard. *Sinclair Lewis*. New York: McGraw-Hill, 1971, Sound, readable treatment of Lewis's life and works. Aimed at younger readers.

Schorer, Mark. *Sinclair Lewis*. Minneapolis: University of Minnesota Press, 1963. A scaled-down, 47-page version of Schorer's 867-page biography, written for the University of Minnesota pamphlet series on American writers.

————. *Sinclair Lewis. A Collection of Critical Essays*. Englewood Cliffs, N.J.: Prentice-Hall, 1962. A chronological arrangement of key critical essays on Lewis by such eminent critics as H. L. Mencken, Joseph Wood Krutch, E. M. Forster, and Malcolm Cowley.

————. *Sinclair Lewis: An American Life*. New York: McGraw-Hill, 1961. The official and indispensable biography, a huge work of enormous energy and insight. Though many have thought his final judgments too harsh, his book remains a model of exhaustive research and incisive prose.

Parts of Books

Geismar, Maxwell. *The Last of the Provincials*, 69–150. Boston: Houghton Mifflin, 1949. One of the best essays on Lewis, this depicts him as a chronicler of American life during its transition from rural to urban settings.

Hoffman, Frederick J. *The Twenties*, 408–15. New York: The Free Press, revised edition, 1962. Sees *Babbitt* as the classic perspective on the American middle class in the 1920s. Hoffman finds the satiric Babbitt and the humane Babbitt poorly combined.

Kazin, Alfred. *On Native Grounds*, 162–180. Garden City, New York: Doubleday Anchor Books, 1956. Authoritative intrepretation of modern American literature, placing Lewis in the tradition of realism.

Kramer, Maurice. "Sinclair Lewis and the Hollow Center." In *The Twenties: Poetry and Prose,* edited by Richard E. Langford and William E. Taylor, 67–69. Deland, Florida: Everett Edwards, 1965. Short but penetrating examination of the problem of how Lewis can be so good and so bad a writer.

Matheson, T. J. "Misused Language: The Narrator's Satiric Function in Sinclair Lewis's *Babbitt.*" In *Sinclair Lewis at 100: Papers Presented at a Centennial Conference,* edited by Michael E. Connaughton, 35–43. St. Cloud, Minnesota: St. Cloud State University, 1985. Insightful analysis of the necessary distortions in Lewis's satire in *Babbitt,* and how this distinguishes his work from standard realism.

Parrington, Vernon Louis. "Sinclair Lewis: Our Own Diogenes." In his *Main Currents in American Thought, vol. III. The Beginnings of Critical Realism in America, 1860–1920,* 360–69. New York: Harcourt, Brace, 1930. An early but still relevant interpretation of Lewis as national irritant, written in a style worthy of Lewis at his best.

Porter, M. Gilbert. "From Babbitt to Rabbit: The American Materialist in Search of a Soul." In *American Literature in Belgium,* edited by Gilbert Debusscher, 185–96. Amsterdam: Rodopi, 1988. Compares Babbitt, Arthur Miller's Willy Loman, and John Updike's Harry "Rabbit" Angstrom as three American salesmen seeking meaning in their lives.

Pugh, David G. "Baedekers, Babbittry and Baudelaire." In *Critical Essays on Sinclair Lewis,* edited by Martin Bucco, 204–13. Boston: G. K. Hall, 1986. Questions whether Lewis's realism in Babbitt, steeped in the popular culture of a past era, can be meaningful to today's readers.

Rourke, Constance. *American Humor,* 22–24. New York: Doubleday Anchor Books, 1953. Sees Lewis as primarily a fabulist, in locating him within the American comic tradition.

Schorer, Mark. "Sinclair Lewis: *Babbitt.*" In *Landmarks of American Writing,* edited by Hennig Cohen, 315–27. New York: Basic Books, 1969. More sympathetic toward Lewis than in his earlier biography, Schorer here celebrates the continuing relevance of *Babbitt.*

Whipple, T. K. "Sinclair Lewis." In his *Spokesmen,* 208–29. New York: D. Appleton, 1928. A shrewd early estimate, centering on what Whipple sees as Lewis's four most pronounced attitudes: satirist, romanticist, philistine, and artist.

Journal Articles

Batchelor, Helen. "A Sinclair Lewis Portfolio of Maps: Zenith to Winnemac." *Modern Language Quarterly* 32 (December 1971): 401–408, plus 20 plates. Reproduces and explains elaborate maps and diagrams Lewis drew while working on *Babbitt*.

Breasted, Charles. "The Sauk-Centricities of Sinclair Lewis." *Saturday Review of Literature* 37 (August 15, 1954): 7–8, 33–35. Memoir covering the years 1922–26. Valuable insights on writing methods of Lewis, and his sense of himself.

Coard, Robert L. "*Babbitt*: The Sound Track of a Satire." *Sinclair Lewis Newsletter* 5–6 (1973–74): 1–4. A linguistic approach emphasizing Lewis's use of alliteration, repetition, and various other devices to suggest the clamor and stridency of modern life.

Davis, Jack. L. "Mark Schorer's *Sinclair Lewis*." *Sinclair Lewis Newsletter* 3 (Spring 1971): 3–9. Davis argues that not until Schorer wrote "Sinclair Lewis: *Babbitt*" in 1969 did he give Lewis full credit for his achievements.

Douglas, George H. "Babbitt at Fifty—The Truth Still Hurts." *The Nation* 214 (May 22, 1972): 661–62. Fair-minded and insightful evaluation of *Babbitt*, fifty years later.

Fisher, Joel. "Sinclair Lewis and the Diagnostic Novel: *Main Street* and *Babbitt*. *Journal of American Studies* 20 (December 1986): 421–33. After cataloging Lewis's faults, Fisher defends Lewis's two novels as the work of "a very acute intellectual hooligan" who diagnoses and analyzes the faults of society.

Hines, Thomas S., Jr. "Echoes from Zenith: Reactions of American Businessmen to *Babbitt*." *Business History Review* 41 (Summer 1967): 123–40. Excellent survey of responses in business magazines to Lewis's portrayal of businessmen in Babbitt. Responses range from anger to praise.

Kallsen, T. J. "The Undeserved Degeneration of 'Babbitt.' " *Names* 21 (June 1973): 124–25. Rightly points out how dictionary definitions of "Babbitt" or "babbitt" exclude the questing side of Babbitt and define him as only a shallow conformist.

Lewis, Robert W. "*Babbitt* and the Dream of Romance." *North Dakota Quarterly* 40 (Winter 1972): 7–14. Sees the search for romantic love as typical of the serious novels of the 1920s, and as the unifying element in *Babbitt*.

Norris, Hoke. "*Babbitt* Revisited." *Yale Review* 68 (1978): 53–70. A retrospective look at *Babbitt*, giving particular attention to describing the popular culture of its time.

Petrullo, Helen B. "*Babbitt* as Situational Satire." *Kansas Quarterly* 1 (Summer 1969): 89–97. Sees much of *Babbitt* as "one degree removed from reality," in following satire's habit of distortion.

Sargent, Marion S. "The Babbitt-Lapham Connection." *Sinclair Lewis Newsletter* 2 (Spring 1970): 8–9. *Babbitt*, like Howells's *The Rise of Silas Lapham*, details a crucial period in the life of a striving businessman.

Schriber, Mary Sue. "You've Come a Long Way, Babbitt! From Zenith to Ilium." *Twentieth Century Literature* 17 (April 1971): 101–06. Convincingly points out many parallels between *Babbitt* and Kurt Vonnegut's *Player Piano*.

Wolfe, Tom. "Stalking the Billion-Footed Beast." *Harper's* 279 (November 1989): 45–56. Spirited call for a return to realism in American writing. Argues for the importance of material to the writer, using Lewis as main example.

Bibliographies

Fleming, Robert E., with Esther Fleming. *Sinclair Lewis: A Reference Guide.* Boston: G. K. Hall, 1980. A thorough annotated bibliography of criticism on Lewis. Invaluable for the serious student of Lewis's works.

———. "A Sinclair Lewis Checklist: 1976–1985." In *Sinclair Lewis at 100,* 267–70. St. Cloud, Minnesota: St. Cloud State University, 1985. Supplements and brings up to 1985 the 1980 Fleming bibliography.

Schorer, Mark. "A Sinclair Lewis Checklist." In his *Sinclair Lewis: An American Life,* 815–26. New York: McGraw-Hill, 1961. A list of items by Lewis and published from 1902 to 1955.

INDEX

Index

THE AUTHOR

Glen A. Love is a professor of English at the University of Oregon, where he teaches and writes on American literature, with emphases on American literary realism, western and northwestern literature, and literature and the environment. His other books include two anthologies, *Contemporary Essays on Prose Style* (with Michael Payne) (1969), and *Northwest Perspectives* (with Edwin R. Bingham) (1979), and a book of criticism, *New Americans: The Westerner and the Modern Experience in the American Novel* (1982). He has taught in Germany, at the universities of Regensburg and Tübingen, under Fulbright grants. He and his wife, Rhoda, a plant ecologist, are active in the environmental movement.